THE UNIVERSITY OF MICHIGAN
CENTER FOR CHINESE STUDIES

MICHIGAN PAPERS IN CHINESE STUDIES

Chang Chun-shu, James Crump, and
Rhoads Murphey, Editors

Ann Arbor, Michigan

The Cultural Revolution: 1967 in Review

Four Essays by:

Michel Oksenberg, Assistant Professor of
Government at Columbia University

Carl Riskin, Assistant Professor of Economics
at Columbia University

Robert A. Scalapino, Professor of Political
Science at the University of California,
Berkeley

Ezra F. Vogel, Professor of Sociology and
Associate Director of the East Asian Center
at Harvard University

Introduction by:

Alexander Eckstein, Professor of Economics
and Director of the Center for Chinese
Studies at the University of Michigan

Michigan Papers in Chinese Studies

No. 2

1968

Open access edition funded by the National Endowment for the Humanities/ Andrew W. Mellon Foundation Humanities Open Book Program.

Copyright 1968

by

Center for Chinese Studies
The University of Michigan
Ann Arbor, Michigan 48104

Printed and bound by CPI Group (UK) Ltd, Croydon, CR0 4YY

ISBN 978-0-89264-002-7 (hardcover)
ISBN 978-0-472-03835-0 (paper)
ISBN 978-0-472-12812-9 (ebook)
ISBN 978-0-472-90212-5 (open access)

Contents

5. THE STRUCTURE OF CONFLICT: CHINA IN 1967

Ezra F. Vogel

Introduction

by

Alexander Eckstein

The four papers in this short symposium volume were prepared for a research conference convened by the University of Michigan Center for Chinese Studies in March 1968. These papers and the conference as a whole were not intended as a detailed or exhaustive account of the course of the Cultural Revolution in Communist China. Although primary emphasis was placed on developments in 1967, the approach was to be topical and analytical rather than chronological and descriptive.

Proceeding on this basis Vogel opens up the discussion by exploring the general structure of the conflict unfolding in China. He then analyzes some of the key issues under contention, examines the factional struggles, and the character of the factions pitted against each other. Oksenberg pursues the problem further by examining the impact of the Cultural Revolution on the following occupational groups in Chinese society: peasants, industrial managers and workers, intellectuals, students, party and government officials, and the military. At the same time, he investigates how each of these key groups affected and shaped the Revolution and the conflicts within it.

While Vogel and Oksenberg are concerned with the impact of the Cultural Revolution on the system as a whole, Riskin and Scalapino analyze its effects on particular segments, i.e. the economy and foreign policy respectively. Riskin explores in particular how it may have affected production trends in agriculture and industry and the movements in foreign trade. He concludes with an appraisal of the Cultural Revolution's economics, i.e. the implications of Maoist economic policies for China's economic growth. Similarly in examing Communist China's foreign policy behavior during this period, Scalapino traces it back to both its Chinese historical roots and to the specific experiences of the Chinese Communist Party. Thus the Chinese Communists in general, and Mao in particular, brought to the process of foreign policy formation a curious combination of cosmic, utopian internationalism and practical ethnocentrism with both rooted in the dual legacy of Chinese tradition and Communist experience.

As is apparent from these papers there are many alternative ways of viewing the origins, the dynamics and the consequences of the Cultural Revolution. Most of our evidence concerning these cataclysmic developments come from the so-called ta tze-pao (wall newspapers) and various Red Guard newspapers of uncertain reliability. Occasionally there are some externally verifiable reports or some bits of objective evidence such as the 30 to 50 disfigured and tied bodies recently washed down into Hong Kong waters. Therefore we will undoubtedly have to wait some time to gain a better perspective on this phase of Communist China's evolution.

In the meantime and on the basis on presently available evidence, it would seem that the Chinese Communist system was from its very inception based on an inherent contradiction and tension which erupted from time to time with the Cultural Revolution merely being its latest and most violent manifestation. Built into the very structure of the system was an inner conflict between the desiderata, the imperatives, and the requirements of technocratic modernization on the one hand and Maoist values and strategy on the other. In a certain sense Maoism can be viewed as totalitarian populism. Just as the Russian populists of the 19th century favored economic development as long as it could be achieved without sacrificing traditional rural-based values, so Mao wants to industrialize China but only if this can be done by keeping the "masses", "the people", permanently mobilized and in a state of permanent revolution. Thus Mao is committed to economic development as long as it can be based on mobilization politics and mobilization economics rather than on technocratic modernization.

One might therefore conclude that Mao would like to see China transformed and modernized without the social and political consequences flowing therefrom. He seems to be particularly concerned about the consequences of functional differentiation, the rise of autonomous interest groups, and the burgeoning of a technocratic bureaucracy be it in the Party, in the Government, or in the Military. This concern is in turn based on a fear that bureaucratization would lead to routinization and a loss of revolutionary élan.

This inner tension and conflict characterizing the system has then significantly contributed to a cyclical pattern of evolution in Communist China. Thus technocratic modernization more or less carried the day during the First Five Year Plan (FFYP) period. Soviet methods of economic planning, Soviet technology in industry, and Soviet military doctrines and weaponry exerted significant influence in China between 1950 and 1957. Apparently frustrated by the lack of agricultural progress and what this might imply for the rest of the economy, the Maoists embarked on the Great Leap in an attempt to substitute mass mobilization techniques for a strategy based on technocratic rationality. Just as the FFYP strategy permeated all aspects of the system, i.e. the Party, the Government, the Army, and the economy, so did the shift to the mobilization strategy of the Great Leap mark a sharp change in policy in all of these spheres. Mobilization entailed growing politicization of the military, of the economy, and of government administration. Moreover, in the military sphere it marked a growing emphasis on a people's war strategy.

As the Great Leap produced a great crisis, Chinese Communist planners were forced by necessity to revert to the path of technocratic modernization in the early 1960's. However, this reversal was never unqualified and was applied much more to economic than to military affairs. This very reversal then produced certain consequences (e.g. disintegration of the communes, weakening of the agricultural collectives, spread of private plots and markets), which must have appeared profoundly disturbing to Mao. Thus the Cultural Revolution may be viewed as Mao's way of counteracting the social and political consequences of economic and other modernization programs following the Great Leap disaster.

Interestingly enough, as Oksenberg suggests, each of these major phases in Communist China's evolution was identified with and carried by one of the three major functional groupings in the country's polity. Thus the technocratic modernization path was pursued and administered during the FFYP period by the government bureaucracy. The mobilization of the highly politicized Great Leap was largely directed by the Communist Party apparatus. With the failure of the Great Leap this apparatus became discredited. Moreover during the great crisis much of its revolutionary élan was dissipated. Therefore if a new mobilization effort was to be launched a new and fresh agent was needed to carry it out. Thus it is not surprising that the principal carrier of the Cultural Revolution became the PLA, which was not primarily responsible either for the FFYP or the Great Leap.

Closely intertwined with these internal policy shifts were certain changes in foreign policy. Scalapino refers to two theories of security as influential in China: one strongly affected by Soviet precepts and the other based on Maoist prescriptions. This had far-reaching effects not only on Sino-Soviet relations, but on the Chinese Communist foreign policy posture as a whole in the 1950's, the early 1960's, and most recently during the Cultural Revolution.

The hypotheses outlined above may be considered as one possible view of the origins of the Cultural Revolution. It more or less represents an interpretation which is either implied or explicitly stated in the four papers. Of course a number of alternative interpretations are possible, which do not necessarily contradict but rather complement the view outlined above. It may not be too far fetched to suggest that at least in part we may be dealing here with an old man syndrome. That is, somewhat like with Stalin, we may be dealing in China with a case of megalomania by an old dictator who has been increasingly losing contact with reality. Perhaps obsessed with a compelling drive to leave a permanently institutionalized legacy of revolution behind him and to push the system rapidly forward in his own lifetime, Mao may have been prepared to initiate and launch the revolution from above at the risk of undermining the very system he helped to build. If this hypothesis is even partially valid, one can not look for significant changes in policy direction until Mao either dies or is somehow neutralized. Correspondingly, it may not be entirely surprising if in years to come we should learn of secret speeches by Mao's successors denouncing him and his deeds. We may very well have to await until that day for a more complete understanding of the Cultural Revolution.

In a more fundamental sense one might look upon the Cultural Revolution as a watershed in the evolution of the Chinese Communist system. In these terms, the power struggles and turmoil of recent years could be viewed as a symptom of cumulative frustration besetting this society and this regime. These frustrations in turn may be arising out of a basic incompatibility between Communist Chinese ambitions and aspirations and their capacities to fulfill them. It must be remembered that the Chinese Communist regime set itself objectives of an unprecedented scope, i.e. they wished to achieve national integration and unity while fostering a socialist revolution, pushing ahead with a forced pace industrialization drive and building a highly centralized order. The enormity of this task is underlined by the fact that all of this is to be done in a highly backward country with the largest population mass in the world and amidst a highly underdeveloped network of communications.

From this vantage point, the Cultural Revolution may be considered as a struggle between those who have come to understand the enormity of this task and are prepared to make the necessary adjustments and compromises either in the pace of advance and/or in the degree of centralized decision-making and others who refuse to face these realities and dilemmas, being convinced that with sufficient revolutionary zeal and commitment the system can surmount all obstacles and move rapidly forward. As of this writing, it would seem that the latter are bound to be disappointed and that their continuing quest may only serve to undermine the very foundations of the system they wanted to build. This proposition is perhaps most clearly dramatized by the fact that under the impact of the Cultural Revolution we see in China today a Communist state with a badly tattered communist party. Without a communist party the whole system not only looses its <u>raison d'étre</u> but its integrating cement. Therefore one might reasonably expect that if the communist system survives the Cultural Revolution it will come out of it much less centralized and in general appreciably transformed.

OCCUPATIONAL GROUPS IN CHINESE SOCIETY AND THE CULTURAL REVOLUTION

Michel Oksenberg*

This paper analyzes the interests and power of seven occupational groups in China: the peasants, industrial workers, industrial managers, intellectuals, students, Party and government bureaucrats, and military personnel. The evidence comes from two sources: 1) the activities of the members of these groups during the Cultural Revolution; and 2) revelations in the wall posters and Red Guard newspapers about their behavior from 1962 to 1966. The paper concludes that the configuration of power and influence among these groups will be an important determinant of Chinese politics in the years ahead.

Analytical Approach

A few years ago, when the totalitarian model of politics in Communist countries was in its heyday, little attention was paid to the ability of various groups in society to influence public policy. The totalitarian model led analysts to concentrate upon the dictator, his whims, the political intrigue among those around him, and the control mechanisms which forced the populace to obey his commands. Barrington Moore and Isaac Deutscher stood out among the analysts of Soviet politics in the early 1950's for their willingness to look beyond Moscow to the power and influence of major groups in society.[1] Now, the totalitarian model has lost its earlier attraction, having proven unable to account for social change. Meanwhile, the approach employed by Moore and Deutscher has begun to win a wider audience, in part because in the early 1950's they suggested the possibilities of significant evolution in the USSR. Recently, Barrington Moore's study of the social origins of democracy and dictator-

*I thank the participants of the "Year-in-Review" seminar for their helpful reactions to a shortened oral presentation of this paper. In addition, I profited from but have not done justice to the comments of several people who read an earlier draft of this paper: Thomas Bernstein, Mark Mancall, Edward Friedman, Robert Packenham, and Lyman VanSlyke. A grant from the East Asian Institute of Columbia University facilitated the typing of the manuscript.

1

ship again has displayed the analytical power of a study of the inter-relationships among key groups in society.[2]

The Cultural Revolution provided a remarkable opportunity to view the structure of Chinese society in the 1960's. Prior to 1965, that view was obscured by the carefully nurtured image of a monolithic society led by a unified, cohesive elite. In 1966-67, the image was destroyed, revealing that the rulers were deeply divided and locked in bitter struggle. As the rulers lost their ability to provide unified, co-herent guidelines to the nation, the various segments of society became more able to pursue their own interests. As a result, the Cultural Revo-lution made it possible to analyze the concerns of the major groups in society and their relative abilities to achieve their interests.

Before the substantive portions of the paper are presented, its analytical framework should be made clear. The analysis has four major conceptual underpinnings. The first concept involves the nature of groups and the ways they are able to articulate their interests. In common parlance, "group" has one of two meanings. One meaning is an "association," a collection of individuals who are formally organized for a purpose. When "interest groups" are discussed in the United States, people have the "association" in mind--a collection of individuals pursuing their common interests in concert. Another definition, more suited to the Chinese case, considers a group to be an aggregate of individuals with similar attributes, roles, or interests. Whether the members of the aggregate become aware of their similarity and form an association depends upon the context. But it is possible for the members of the aggregate, acting separately, to behave in the same way because of the similarity of their positons. In these terms, then, peasants can react to government policy as a group, that is, as an aggregate of indi-viduals making similar decisions.

A second concept embodied in the analysis is that unorganized groups or aggregates can affect the policy formulation process. In democratic countries, aggregates have little trouble forming associations and gaining access to the key centers of decision making. In non-demo-cratic countries, aggregates continue to pursue their interests, but since they are unable to organize, they must adopt different techniques. Manipulation of information, passive resistance, non-compliance, and cultivation of friends in high places of government are some of the in-direct methods which enable groups to influence policy. The important research question, as far as China is concerned, is to determine how and to what extent each aggregate registers its demands.

A third aspect of the analysis is that some groups in society have a greater ability than others to influence policy. A number of factors determine what groups have the greatest power, but key among them are the degree of their organization, the relationship of these groups to the means of production, the values and attitudes of the particular culture, the international situation, and the interrelationship among various groups. The process of industrialization involves the removal, often violently, of some groups from the locus of power, and their replacement by new groups.

Finally, the fourth underpinning of group analysis is the notion that, to a considerable extent, politics involves the attempts by powerless groups to obtain power, while groups with power struggle to retain it. Moreover, the politics of a country to a large extent reflects the conflicts within the groups that have power. In societies where the military has power, for example, national politics comes to involve interservice rivalries, conflicts between senior and junior officers, and disputes between central headquarters and regional commands. If one can chart the distribution of power among various groups in a society, then one can predict what some of the important public policies and political issues will be.

The application of these concepts to the events in China in 1966-67 must not be misinterpreted as an attempt to explain the Cultural Revolution. Rather, this paper analyzes the Cultural Revolution for what it tells about one aspect of the structure of Chinese society. The seven broad occupational groups into which the Chinese Communists divide their society--peasants, intellectuals, industrial managers, industrial workers, students, Party and government bureaucrats, and the military--are examined briefly and crudely, with the following questions in mind: What were some of the salient characteristics of these groups? What did the members of these aggregates perceive to be in their interest? Did the aggregates have any common group interests, and if so, what were they? How did they pursue their interests? What power did they have to enforce their demands?

These questions are not easily answered. Without the opportunity to do field research, it is difficult to ascertain what people perceive to be in their interests. The activities of the members of different occupational groups during 1966-67 and statements in the wall posters and Red Guard newspapers about their attitudes and behavior provide some clues. In addition, occupational groups appear to have some similar characteristics, no matter what country is under investigation; the literature on the roles and behavior of members of these groups in the developing countries then provides inferences about some of their likely interests in China. Further, some information is available on the perceived interests of different occupational groups in pre-Communist China. By seeking convergence among the different sources of information, the analyst can roughly identify occupational group interests at the present time. It is harder to estimate the ability of these aggregates to articulate their interests and affect public policy, but surely the relevant data here include actual instances of members of these groups influencing important political decisions or public policy clearly reflecting the interests of the group.

An analysis of the activities of occupational groups during the Cultural Revolution admittedly provides only a limited perspective upon the extraordinarily complex events of 1966-67. But no single vantage will suffice in interpreting history of such sweeping proportions. Some of the valuable perspectives employed in other essays on the Cultural Revolution and purposefully eschewed here include analysis in terms of elites,[3] bureaucratic phenomena,[4] problems of industrialization,[5] and the Chinese political culture.[6] By approaching the Cultural Revolution from the perspective of occupational group interests, one of the oldest methods of political analysis, one hopefully will acquire additional insights into the structure of Chinese society and its relationship to the Chinese political system.

Peasants

Peasant Interests. An important desire of most peasants probably is to be free to cultivate, reap, market, and consume their crops; they wish to have less extracted from them, and more goods available for purchase at lower prices. Peasants particularly demand political quietude during the planting and harvesting seasons. They also want their government to protect them from disorder and the ravages of nature. In addition, to the extent that their aspirations have risen, China's peasants also want better educational opportunities for their children, more welfare, greater security, and a standard of living comparable to urban dwellers.

Articulation of Peasant Interests. Peasants have no associations to voice their demands. Nonetheless, the Cultural Revolution provided ample evidence that the peasants had brokers embodying and representing their interests. Recalling the disaster of the Great Leap, when peasant desires had been disregarded, many among the Peking leadership strove to anticipate peasant reaction to proposed policies. Moreover, upon occasion, outbreaks of violence in the countryside forced the officials to pay attention to peasant grievances.

The brokers came primarily from three sources: the officials in agricultural agencies, regional officials whose power stemmed in part from the performance of agriculture in their areas, and military officers. A number of leading agricultural officials, in particular Teng Tzu-hui, T'an Chen-lin, and Liao Lu-yen, were accused in the ta-tze-pao of seeking to expand private plots and free markets, to restrict the power of the communes, and to assign brigade plots to individual households, thereby restoring production responsibility to the family.

Teng, T'an, and Liao, in effect, were voicing the interests of their peasant constituents. The reason for their action seems clear. The performance of the agencies which they led was judged largely by agricultural production. They depended upon the peasants to fulfill the targets for which the agencies were held responsible. It was in their interest, therefore, to argue for measures and to secure targets congruent with peasant interests.

Similarly, regional officials occasionally represented the interests of the peasants in their area. The purge of Li Ching-ch'uan of Szechuan has proven fascinating in this regard. If the charges against him are accurate, Li was keenly aware of the peculiarities of the Szechuan agricultural system, and sought to win exemptions from the uniform, nationwide regulations Peking sought to impose. He took exception, for example, to marketing regulations which Mao had endorsed. He pointed out that (because of the terrain and scattered population) rural markets in Szechuan were different from the rest of the country. [7]

The military also had a vested interest in peasant morale. To the People's Liberation Army fell the unpleasant task of suppressing peasant unrest. Moreover, soldiers were recruited in the countryside, and troop morale was adversely affected by disenchantment at home. [8] The PLA conducted periodic surveys of troop morale, and monitored letters from home. When the surveys and monitoring revealed disenchantment at home, the military command apparently voiced its concern. As a result of these channels of communication, some military officers became particularly sensitive to the problems of the peasants and upon occasion acted as their representative. This is precisely what P'eng Teh-huai was doing at Lushan in 1959 when he expressed the discontent of the peasants with the commune system. [9]

In addition to representation by brokers, peasants acted on their own behalf. Such actions included failure to comply with directives--for example, hiding production and concentrating on private plots--and sporadic violence. The Work Bulletin described peasant violence in Honan province in 1960, while during the first half of 1967 there were persistent reports of small peasant uprisings and of an illegal influx of peasants into many Chinese cities. [10]

These means of voicing their interests, when combined with surveys measuring rural discontent and the visits by higher level officials to the countryside, added up to a general awareness in Peking of the desires and problems of the peasants.

Sources of Peasant Strength and Weaknesses. The power of the peasants to enforce their demands, however, was limited by the fact that they had no organization which could be considered their own. One wall poster indicated that some peasants were acutely aware of this problem:

> Workers have their unions, soldiers have theirs,
> and Party workers have a body to represent their
> interests. Why don't we have unions?....
> The peasants have no voice. They have only
> 'formal' democracy. At the Second Conference of
> our Poor and Lower Middle Peasants Association,
> no decisions were made by us. All we had was a
> few days of free board and lodging. [11]

As anthropologists stress, peasants must overcome innumerable difficulties to become an organized, articulate, enduring political force. [12] Concerned with sheer survival and possessing only limited horizons, most peasants enter the political process rarely or not at all. They must depend upon sympathetic brokers to transmit their concerns to those who control the resources they want; barring that, their only recourse is non-compliance or violence.

This is particularly true in China, where the peasants are now bonded to the land. Owning only a small percentage of the land they till, unable to move without a hard-to-obtain permit, forced to deposit savings in state-regulated credit cooperatives which restrict withdrawals, peasants are largely at the mercy of lower level Party and government bureaucrats.

But it is easy to underestimate the power of the peasant aggregate. China's rulers must be at least somewhat responsive to the demands of the peasants because of their numbers (roughly 80% of the population) and their economic importance. Roughly 35% to 45% of China's net domestic product, for example, comes from the agricultural sector, and the bulk of China's exports are agricultural and agriculturally derived products. [13]

The Cultural Revolution demonstrated that political power still was rooted to a considerable degree in control over the peasants and agricultural surpluses. The purges of Li Ching-ch'uan, the powerful Szechuan official, and T'ao Chu, the former Kwangtung official, show how these men were somewhat responsive to peasant demands in order to encourage the peasants to develop the potential of their areas. On the other hand, officials in grain-deficit areas, more dependent upon allocations from central government storehouses, were less able to resist Peking directives. Heilungkiang, Shantung, Shansi, Kweichow, Tsinghai, Peking, and Shanghai--all grain-deficit areas--were among the first to respond to Peking's call in early 1967 to establish Revolutionary Committees. (There undoubtedly were other reasons for their response.) Here are indications of the persistence in China of the intimate relationship between power and agriculture. The peasant has not yet lost his crucial role as a source of bureaucratic power.

Peasants During the Cultural Revolution. The course of the Cultural Revolution indicates that by 1967 even the radicals were somewhat sensitive to peasant needs. The two strongest efforts to subdue the Cultural Revolution came precisely at those moments when the peasants probably most desired order. Although earlier efforts had been made, the Red Guards were finally told to cease their marches and return home in early February 1967 on the eve of the spring planting. The PLA received more vigorous orders than usual to assist the peasants in spring planting. These February directives, coming on the heels of widespread signs of peasant unrest, were issued only 45 days after the December 15th directive extending the Cultural Revolution to the countryside. [14] This apparently calmer situation prevailed until early summer, when the turmoil increased. As the fall harvest neared, however, the Peking authorities again recognized the constraints imposed by China's essentially rural character; in late August and early September, they took stringent measures to control the Cultural Revolution. [15]

The peasant desire to be left alone was recognized in other ways. There is remarkably little evidence that the agitational activity which marked the Cultural Revolution in the urban areas spread to the country-side.[16] To judge from the provincial radio broadcasts, the main under-taking of the Cultural Revolution in the countryside was the propagation of Mao's thought, primarily through the organization of Mao-study groups. In spite of all the condemnations, there were very few reports of actual seizure of the private plots or restriction of free markets. The announce-ments of a good harvest in 1967 further reflected the fact that the Cul-tural Revolution essentially had by-passed the rural areas. In short, the evidence strongly suggests that the interests of the peasants elicit a response from China's rulers.

Industrial Managers and Industrial Workers

Since the divergent interests of industrial managers and workers are what strike most Americans, it is wise to recall their common inter-ests in China. Both usually have a vested interest in uninterrupted pro-duction, in protecting factory equipment from damage, and in maintain-ing industrial prosperity and growth. In China, both have a vested in-terest in the evolving factory management system, in view of the welfare and housing benefits it bestows upon them. Moreover, the deep economic depression following the Great Leap very possibly had underscored to many the commonality of manager and worker interests in resisting at-tempts by other groups to intrude upon their domain. In spite of com-mon interests, however, industrial manager and worker have rarely joined together to influence the course of Chinese politics.

Against this background, the events from December 1966 to February 1967 assume historical significance. They suggest that China's industrial sector has begun to come of political age. With a few excep-tions, the industrial managers and workers, apparently acting in concert, resisted the efforts by parts of the bureaucracy and organized students to intrude upon areas they deemed to be their prerogatives. Within one month of the decision to extend the Cultural Revolution to the factories, the order was quietly but significantly tempered. If China's rulers had been unified in their support of the spread of the Cultural Revolution to the factories, the ability of the industrial managers and workers to tem-per its course would have been questionable. But the move was initiated only by a radical segment within the Party and government bureaucracy, who required student support. More noteworthy, the considerable op-position within the bureaucracy indicated that since the Great Leap, the industrial managers and workers had acquired strong allies among the top officials.

The exact story of industrial cities in late 1966 and early 1967 has yet to be told, but enough is known to warrant a brief description. [17] In the stormy period following the August 1966 Eleventh Plenum, the Red Guards were repeatedly told that they were not to enter factories without prior approval of the factory employees, nor to interfere with production. One of the strongest warnings came in a November 10, 1966, People's Daily editorial, which said,

> Revolutionary students should firmly believe that the worker and peasant masses are capable of making revolution and solving their problems by themselves. No one should do their work for them. Special attention must also be paid to preventing interference with production activities... from the outside. [18]

But by December 9, the earlier policy was reversed and a more radical policy was adopted; the Red Guards were encouraged to enter the factories. In early December, in contrast to the November 10th editorial, a Red Guard newspaper could state,

> Chairman Mao has taught us, 'The Young intellectuals and young students of China must definitely go among the worker and peasant masses...' The cultural revolutionary movement must expand from the young people and students to the workers and peasants. [19]

The formal decision allowing the students to enter the factories, promulgated on December 9, was made public in the important People's Daily editorial of December 26th. [20]

Five days later, the annual People's Daily New Year editorial indicated that there was considerable opposition to the measure. The editorial stated, "Any argument against carrying out a large-scale cultural revolution in factories and mines and in rural areas is not correct." [21] According to the rules of Pekingology, this sentence indicates that a strong debate was being waged. Moreover, by mid-January it was clear that the industrial managers and workers were undermining the December 9th directive. Rather than allowing the Red Guards to enter the factories, which might have led to damage of equipment, the factory managers encouraged their employees to leave the factories and travel to Peking to voice their grievances. Factory managers paid bonuses to their workers,

promoted many of them, and gave them travel fare. Protesting Red
Guard activities, it appears, factory workers went on strike, probably
living off the bonuses paid them by their factory managers.

The joint activities of managers and workers, assisted by
some Party and government bureaucrats, were described in an "Open
Letter" which stated:

> In recent days..., a handful of freaks and
> monsters have cheated the misled...worker
> masses, to put forward many wage, welfare,
> and other economic demands to the leadership
> and administrative departments... These admini-
> strative departments and leaders, acceeding to
> these demands and not caring whether it is in
> accord with state policy or not, sign their names
> to hand out generously a lot of state funds. 22

Those who encouraged the workers to put forth their economic demands
were accused of setting the "revolutionary workers movement onto the
devious road of trade unionism. "

The situation in Shanghai became particularly critical. The
railroad network was partially paralyzed due to a high rate of employee
absenteeism, with serious disruptions from December 27 to January 9.
Public utility services in Shanghai were disrupted; shipping in the Shanghai harbor was adversely affected. Similar reports came from throughout the country. By mid-January, Radio Peking and the New China News
Agency (NCNA) had reported instances of worker's strikes and sabotage
in such major cities as Tientsin, Shenyang, Chengtu, Chungking, Sian,
Canton, and Hangchow.

Within a month of the December 9th directive, the radical
attack upon the industrial sector had produced near-chaos. The first
response of the leaders of the radical Party and government bureaucrats
and their Red Guard student supporters was to win allies among the
workers and to encourage conflict between managers and workers. Special appeals were made to the temporary factory employees (Factories
have two types of employees on their pay roll--permanent employees,
who are paid according to the set wage scale, receive fringe benefits,
and have a regular rank; and temporary employees, who are employed
on special contract, receive lower wages, and can be dismissed easily
during a recession). To gain the favor of the temporary employees, the

radicals blamed Liu Shao-ch'i for originating the temporary employee
system. They implied that one of the purposes of the Cultural Revolution was to abolish the distinction between permanent and temporary
labor. At the same time, the radicals attempted to isolate the factory
managers from their worker allies. The managers were attacked as
anti-Maoists; the workers were excused for being duped. A series of
student-worker meetings was arranged to build good will.

The tacit alliance, particularly between managers and permanent employees, held firm and the government had to take stringent
measures to restore industrial production. On January 15, Chou En-lai
cautioned the Red Guards against hasty action. He implied that the
action in Shanghai was too rash, adding that "we must.... see to it that
business organizations truly carry out business operations."[23] Two days
later, the CCP Central Committee and State Council jointly issued regulations to strengthen urban public security work,[24] On January 28th,
an article by Mao Tse-tung entitled "On Correcting Mistaken Ideas in
the Party," stressing the virtues of discipline and order, was reprinted,
while on the next day, the State Council prohibited industrial workers
from visiting their rural ancestral homes during the Chinese New Year.
The efforts to keep the workers in the city, to keep the chaos in the
cities from spreading to the countryside, and to restore urban order
were receiving primary attention. To win back the permanent employees,
on February 17 the Central Committee and the State Council decided to
retain the distinction between permanent and temporary workers.

The stringent measures did not produce immediate results.
They were intended to restore the confidence of the industrial worker,
but they did little to assuage the fears of the factory managers, former
capitalists, trade union leaders, and economic planners. The industrial
sector apparently did not begin to return to normal until these groups
also were mollified. To restore industrial calm, the vehement charges
of "economism" levelled against the industrial managers began to be
dampened in February. The press concentrated its attack upon "anarch-
ists," meaning the Red Guards who persisted in their attacks on managers.
The slogan so prominent in December and early January, "To Rebel is
Justified," gave way to expressions of concern for the sanctity of property.

In view of the tacit manager-worker alliance, and the initial
attempts both to split this alliance and divide the workers, the CCP
Central Committee letter of March 18 has very special importance. Ad-
dressed jointly to the industrial workers and their leaders, the document

officially recognized their common interests. Extremely mild in tone, the letter represents an almost total abandonment of the policy outlined in the December 26, 1966 People's Daily editorial extending the Cultural Revolution to the factories. The support given to the factory managers in the March 18 directive is worth quoting:

> As masters of the country, all workers and staff in factories and mines must, in the course of the Cultural Revolution, heighten their great sense of responsibility and protect State property effectively...
> The Party Central Committee believes that in all factories and mines, the majority of cadres are good or relatively good. (emphasis mine)[25]

The mere issuance of these instructions did not restore industrial peace. The PLA also was instructed to enter factories to maintain discipline.[26] Workers who had joined the radicals were difficult to control, and factional strife among workers was a frequent phenomenon. Reports of worker absenteeism persisted. The effort to put factory production on a firm footing remained an elusive goal for the rest of the year.

Although these developments were important, the main significance of the events in China's cities from December, 1966 to February, 1967 should not be lost. In the heat of the Cultural Revolution, the industrial managers and workers, acting together, were able to alter drastically the intended course of the Cultural Revolution. The working class and their managers have moved closer to the center of power in Chinese politics.

Intellectuals

In the broadest terms, intellectuals have three tasks. First, they pass the values and accumulated knowledge from one generation to another. Second, they increase the sum total of knowledge and create new works of art. Third, intellectuals criticize the society in which they live and point out alternative ways of ordering their society. Intellectuals can be distinguished according to the relative emphasis they place upon these roles. Thus, the teacher primarily transmits the knowledge of his generation to his students. The nuclear physicist is responsible for providing new information. The political satirist criticizes his society.

Depending upon the values of the society and the demands of the most powerful groups in the political arena, the particular roles performed by intellectuals command somewhat different rewards.[27] The Cultural Revolution demonstrated the political value of each of these roles in China.

Social Critic. The social critic was totally vulnerable to political control, as the attacks upon Wu Han and the Three Family Village with which he was associated revealed. To recall briefly, the historian Wu Han wrote on the virtues of the Ming minister Hai Jui.[28] Hai Jui had criticized a Ming emperor's alleged neglect of the peasants, and was removed from office as a result. Mao Tse-tung and those around him charged that Wu Han was using the story of Hai Jui as an allegory to attack Mao and defend P'eng Teh-huai, the dismissed Minister of Defense who had also protested against his leader's peasant policy. Mao, in short, was able to remove Wu Han and others after demonstrating that they were playing the role of social critic. This is not surprising for a society in which the distinction between criticism and disloyalty has often been blurred.

Transmitters of Values and Knowledge. The Cultural Revolution also showed that the transmitters of values and knowledge serve at the pleasure of the dominant political groups. As Mao's earlier optimism about the fate of the communist revolution gave way to a more pessimistic appraisal, he became more concerned with the educational process. While optimistic, he could afford to be lenient toward the past, for he believed China would not remain its captive. Later, the accumulated knowledge of the past and those who propagated it became threatening.

Several factors help to explain the political weakness of the propagandists, teachers, artists, and other transmitters of culture and knowledge. First, they had no economic allies, for few people's livelihoods depended upon them. Second, they were divided internally. Some younger "transmitters," such as the idealogues who came to the fore in late 1966--Wang Li, Yao Wen-yuan, Ch'i Pen-yu, and Kuan Feng--apparently were ready to assist in the removal of their superiors. Third, many "transmitters" had strong enemies among their students. Initially, the weight of tradition and knowledge and its concommitant responsibilities rests heavy upon students, and they tend to resent those who place it upon them. Students therefore were ready allies of the political groups who attacked the propagandists and teachers.

Researchers. At the very moment the critics were condemned and the teachers were attacked, the press pointedly praised other intellectuals for developing nuclear weaponry, synthesizing insulin, and improving medical techniques.[29] The increasing importance of China's scientific community enables this segment of the intellectuals to exert its claims. A reasonable assumption is that many scientists are willing to recognize the supremacy of any political leader, so long as they are able to pursue their intellectual interests. This seems to be the tacit bargain struck during the Cultural Revolution. In the 1966-67 reports of their work, scientists always paid homage to the inspiration they derived from Chairman Mao. In exchange, Mao appears to have made fewer demands upon the time of scientists during this campaign than he did during the Great Leap Forward. For example, the twelfth point of the Sixteen Point Central Committee Directive on the Cultural Revolution specifically exempted the scientists, stating:

> As regards scientists, technicians, and ordinary members of working staffs, as long as they are patriotic, work energetically, are not against the Party and socialism, and maintain no illicit relations with any foreign country, we should in the present movement continue to apply the policy of 'unity, criticism, unity.' Special care should be taken of those scientists and scientific and technical personnel who have made contributions. [30]

Among China's intellectuals, the scientists fared best in 1966-67. Unlike peasants, industrial managers, or workers, who were able to defend their interests only after an initial attack against them, the scientists saw their interests taken into account prior to the Cultural Revolution. Since their role in China's industrialization effort is valued by other groups in society, they appear to have representation at the center of power.

Students

The Cultural Revolution suggests that Chinese students in many ways resemble students everywhere, particularly in the underdeveloped world. Four tendencies among Chinese students seem particularly noteworthy: idealism, deep ambivalence toward authority, highly developed consciousness of their student identity, and low capacity to form associations. These four characteristics must be analyzed at greater length.

Student Idealism. With respect to their idealism, Seymour Lipset put it well in a general essay on the topic: "Educated young people...tend disproportionately (to their numbers) to support idealistic movements which take the ideologies and values of the adult world more seriously than does the adult world itself."[31] Lipset's observation seems applicable to China. During the Cultural Revolution, as during the Hundred Flowers Campaign of 1957, the students did not reject the ideals of the adult world, but rather criticized adults for not practicing their ideals. Moreover, as Lipset would predict, many Chinese students adamantly refused to compromise on matters they deemed of principle. Theirs was a movement in pursuit of the millennium.

Several factors seem to have produced their radicalism, not the least of which was that the students had been the target of intensive ideological campaigns, especially from 1962 on. The majority of the Red Guards it should be remembered, were the first total products of the Chinese Communist educational system.[32] The values transmitted in these schools, glorifying revolution and Mao Tse-tung, apparently had an impact.

Another reason for student radicalism was their limited stake in the status quo. The Red Guards drew a particularly enthusiastic response not from college students but from the younger, middle school students, precisely the segment of youth which had invested the least time and effort in planning a career. Moreover, in the Chinese cultural context, students can more easily afford to be radical than adults because of their more limited familial obligations. Certainly one of the striking and credible revelations during the Cultural Revolution concerns the familial interests of the older cadres in China. As they matured and assumed demanding adult roles, the former student radicals of the 1920's and 1930's, acting as good Chinese, paid increasing attention to the fortunes of their families. They made sure that their descendents received a good education, and even established special schools for the families of cadres. They saw to it that their children married into decent families and obtained good jobs.[33] And in many instances, the revolutionary leaders of China seem to have enjoyed close, warm relations with their children and grandchildren. These concerns apparently sapped their revolutionary zeal, for rapid social change would have made it impossible for them to assure the continuity of their family. This may be one of the major reasons why students have been so important in China's radical movements. Away from home, with neither children nor dependent parents, students were relatively unencumbered by the net of mutual obligations which confine adult Chinese. They were free to be radical.

<u>Ambivalent Attitudes of Students Toward Older Generation.</u>
Another characteristic of students, their tendency to regard the older
generation with deep ambivalence, also helps to explain their idealism
and zealotry. On the one hand, the Cultural Revolution indicated that
many students seek the emotional support and intellectual guidance of
an older authority figure. On the other hand, the Cultural Revolution
also showed that many students tend to regard the older generation with
distrust. In China, as elsewhere, a generational gap has developed.
Some of the causes of the gap can be identified.

Many students apparently resented the fact that the older
generation had the jobs and power which they wanted. The Red Guards
concentrated their attacks upon those parts of the bureaucracy which
had been most reluctant to promote youth. According to some refugee
informants, the Party apparatus--particularly the secretariat on each
governmental level and the Organization Department--placed the greatest
stress upon seniority as a criterion for employment and promotion. [34]
At the same time, the PLA and the finance and trade fields appear to
have been more willing to reward youth. The PLA, with its "up or out"
promotion system, guarantees to its younger members opportunities for
upward mobility in the organization. The finance and trade system, expanding with the economy, probably was somewhat more able to offer
employment opportunities to students. Not surprisingly, then, while
the students were quick to "bombard the headquarters" of the Party
apparatus, they were less concerned with bureaucratism in the PLA
and the finance and trade system. In sum, their zealous conduct toward
the older generation partly reflected a frustration in employment opportunities.

But this was not the only source of generational tensions. The
Cultural Revolution also indicated that many Chinese students resented
their elders placing unwanted responsibilities on their shoulders. Urban
students in particular began to feel these burdens in their high school
days, as they first contemplated the problems of career, marriage,
filial obligations, and maintenance of traditions. The student violence
toward both teachers and parents in July and August, 1966 underscored
the hostility with which youth viewed those in charge of disciplining them. [35]

Yet another cause of the generational tensions was the different environments in which the older generation and the students were
reared. Many older cadres, Mao included, viewed the younger generation

with apprehension, fearful that their education in a peaceful China did
not imbue them with a spirit of self-sacrifice and dedication to change.[36]
Students also were keenly aware of the gap that separated them from the
older revolutionary generation. As early as 1963, an article in the journal China Youth put the problem as seen by youth quite well:

> In discussing heroic persons, frequently one
> hears many youth say such things as, 'The era
> creates heroes.' 'Only when a drop of water
> flows down a mountain can it become part of a
> wave. Our lives are in an era of peaceful con-
> struction. We are water on a plain and only can
> advance slowly and quietly.'
> The feelings go to such lengths that some
> youth believe they were born at an unfortunate time.
> They say, "If I were born thirty years earlier, I
> certainly would have participated in the Long
> March; if I were born twenty years earlier, I
> certainly would have been a hero in the anti-Jap-
> anese war. If I were ten years older, I cer-
> tainly would have compiled a war record in Korea.'[37]

This passage points both to the generational gap which youth
perceived, and more significantly, to their desire to narrow that gap.
In other words, the above quotation reveals the eagerness of some youths
to seize an opportunity to "make revolution," and thereby to join the
portion of the older generation whose exploits they admire. Under the
communists as well as in traditional times, Chinese moral education
makes considerable use of models whom students are taught either to
follow or shun.[38] Teenagers are conditioned to search for model men
to emulate, and they search for models among older men as well as
among youth. Thus, the ambivalent attitude of students toward the older
generation becomes understandable. While they resented the burdens the
elders place upon them, they depended upon the elders to provide them
with models of moral action.[39]

Many students in China, the Red Guards' experience suggests,
adopted the model of the Chinese revolutionary tradition, with the roman-
ticism and heroism they associated with it. In this, they follow Mao.
Leaders who successfully associated themselves with this tradition and
who were sympathetic to problems of youth acquired student support. On
the other hand, the students seemed prone to reject the adult's world of
bureaucracy, which to them meant examinations and the need to plan
careers. They considered as negative examples the men who, they were

told, were responsible for bureaucracy - Liu Shao-ch'i, Teng Hsiao-p'ing, P'eng Chen, et. al.

The accounts of Chou En-lai's appearances among the students give the impression of a leader who successfully bridged the generational gap and enjoyed a special rapport with the students. (His support among the students in the early days of the Cultural Revolution, in turn, may have added to his power within leadership circles.) One such account told of a Chou En-lai visit to Tsinghua University. Displaying magnificent command of Mandarin, Chou stated:

> In regard to your school, only by coming into
> your midst will one penetrate the masses. Never-
> theless, now that I have come, I am still barely
> scratching the surface. (Audience: No!) No? I
> am sincere, let us think it over. If I do not go to
> your class room, your dormitory, and your dining
> room, how can I dissolve the unnecessary estrange-
> ment, unnecessary oppostion, and unnecessary mis-
> understanding among you? Yet, you may ask me:
> Why are you so selfish? I am not! It is not being
> selfish. I feel bad that the problems were not solved
> satisfactorily by my talk last time. .....I heard
> that, after my talk here last time, your problems
> were not satisfactorily solved, and that you posted
> three large-letter bulletins about me. They were
> too few. Reading over my speech again, I feel that
> you did not post enough large-letter bulletins. Many
> of your suggestions are correct.
>   I wish to discuss my views once more. One
> must ceaselessly examine oneself. As I already
> mentioned last time, one must work, learn, and re-
> form all one's life. [40]

The speech was delivered in a rain, but Chou apparently refused offers to hold an umbrella over him, saying, "You gave me a Red Guard arm badge. Similar to you, we also steel ourselves in the great storms." At the end of his talk, Chou led the students in singing of "Sailing the Seas Depends on the Helmsman." His was a masterful performance of a 68-year-old man successfully bridging the generational gap. The response he elicited is testimony to the importance of this aspect of the problem of youth in China today.

Student Consciousness. A third aspect of student life made
evident in the Cultural Revolution was its intensity. College students
and even many high school students lived on large campuses; their
dormitories were crowded. In the suburbs of Peking, for example, several large university campuses were in close proximity. In such an environment, as at large American universities, students had little contact
with faculty. They formed their own community, and acquired a high
consciousness of their identity as students. In fact, some of Marx's
observations about the sources of working-class consciousness are applicable to the rise of student consciousness: large numbers of people
massed together, in similar positions, having a high rate of interaction.
In addition, Chinese students, particularly those attending Peking University and Tsinghua University, were aware of the role of their prede-
cessors in the May Fourth and December Ninth movements. It was
therefore, in a sense, natural for the students to respond, as a group,
to Mao's initial call for a student movement.

Moreover, student self-awareness probably was intensified
during 1966-67. Group consciousness tends to be heightened by the
kind of conflict that students experienced in 1966-67. In addition, student consciousness probably developed as their parochial, regional
loyalties were weakened through the nationwide marches and "linking
up" activities.

Student Inability to Organize. A fourth characteristic, an especially fascinating aspect of the Cultural Revolution, was the students' inability to form effective associations, in spite of the constant exhortations
to do so. Intense factional disputes marked Red Guard activities almost
from their inception. While the issues involved in the disputes are not
entirely clear, in part they appear to reflect the factional strife among
the elite. Mao and the group around him organized Red Guard groups
in the summer of 1966 to assist them in their attacks upon perceived
enemies in the Party and government bureaucracy. Very soon thereafter, other officials began organizing Red Guard groups loyal to them.

As the conflicts between these Red Guard groups intensified
and spread throughout the country, particularly from January to August,
1967, it apparently became possible for other students to form their
own, unaffiliated organizations. The students of China, accustomed to
a highly structured environment, suddenly found themselves in a near-
chaotic situation. Previously, students were told which organizations

were good, which were bad; they had little choice in organizational affiliations. Now, they had to choose among virtually indistinguishable organizations, recognizing that the wrong affiliation could ruin their careers. Little wonder, then, that in such an environment, with little previous experience in forming associations, the students failed miserably. They rapidly degenerated into quarreling, disruptive groups. Unaccustomed to the process of compromise and decision, debates over seemingly trivial issues apparently quickly became problems symbolic of the struggle between the two roads of capitalism and socialism. Coercion became the only way to re-establish order among the youth. The PLA dispatched units to schools; several young rowdies were executed in stadiums and the spectacle televised.

Another related phenomenon also appeared at this time. Unable to associate effectively, some youths simply withdrew from any political activity. Withdrawal apparently was widespread enough to deserve comment from one of Shanghai's leading papers, Wen-hui Pao. An editorial in the paper stated:

> There has emerged a number of people who do not pay attention to state affairs and who remain outside the revolutionary movement. These people can be called wanderers.
> They are people who entertain the attitude of non-intervention toward the life-and-death struggle between the proletariat and the bourgeoisie. Whenever they are required to reveal their attitude, they usually just issue a vague statement. Instead of fighting.... they wander around school campuses, parks, and streets... They pay no attention to proletarian politics and become dispassionate onlookers.
> Some are the so-called veteran rebels who, after a long period of time, became tired of the civil wars among the mass organizations to which they belonged. Instead of seeking ways to stop civil wars and fighting the common enemy, they flew the flag of truce in order to avoid trouble. [41]

The editorial confirms a predictable development. The Red Guards were intended in part to build a sense of community among youth. While undoubtedly becoming more conscious of their identity, instead of acquiring a sense of belonging, the youth probably became more aware of their isolation and their inability to form associations. Moreover, unattainable expectations were probably aroused among some youth in the course of the Cultural Revolution. The sense of isolation and the disappointments appear to have led to alienation or anomie rather than to commitment, the Wen-hui Pao editorial suggests.

Students during the Cultural Revolution. With the four characteristics of Chinese youth as revealed during 1966-67 -- their radicalism, ambivalence toward authority, sense of identity, and low capability of association -- it is now possible to summarize the ability of the students to affect public policy during the Cultural Revolution. At the outset, the eager students were easily mobilized to attack the bureaucrats in the culture and education system. This occurred by September, 1966. Mao and his associates saw that they had forged a powerful organizational weapon. The brutal Red Guard attacks upon defenseless victims in August and September, 1966, however, soon made clear that the weapon would not be easily controlled. The mass rallies held from August to October in Peking were perhaps envisioned as a method for providing the youth with an emotional catharsis that would reduce their lust for violence. [42] At the same time, the energy of the youth was tapped by Mao and the radicals around him to attack provincial level Party organizations throughout the country.

But for tens of millions of youths demanding participation in revolutionary activity, the dragging out of a couple hundred provincial and municipal level Party secretaries only whetted the appetite. The youth appear to have kept pressing for more and bigger targets. In early December, 1966, as mentioned earlier, the industrial sector was opened, while on December 15, the rural sector was opened. With the resistance encountered in both these sectors, they were removed from the list of targets in late January. The leaders of China cast about for diversionary targets and in February and March, foreign embassies in Peking bore the brunt of Red Guard hostility. But this too had its limits. Several foreign countries were in no mood to tolerate such diplomatic outrages. In March, the target was narrowed to Liu Shao-ch'i, Teng Hsiao-p'ing, T'ao Chu, and the other "top Party persons in authority taking the capitalist road." At the same time, students were encouraged to return to school.

The rebellious force which the leaders had unleashed eight months earlier was not easy to contain, however. In search of new targets, the more radical students next wanted to take on the army. One reason for the increased animosity among many students toward the army was the role it played in quelling factional strife among youth. Following the

July defiance of Peking's orders by the Wuhan garrison commander Ch'en Tsai-tao, students apparently increased the pressure to be given the army as a target; some of the ultra-radicals in Mao's entourage supported the student demands. In late August this target was firmly denied to them and new efforts were then made to open schools. By late fall, 1967, the Red Guards were less frequently in the news, and in January, 1968, a call came for a rectification campaign in Red Guard organizations. The main youth organization prior to the advent of the Red Guards, the Communist Youth League (CYL), rarely mentioned during 1967, began to be mentioned again in early 1968. The radical student movement had run its course, and an effort was being made to re-establish control over youth. In sum, youth were on the periphery of the political arena prior to mid-1966, had been allowed to enter the center by the radicals to wreak their havoc and steel themselves in revolution in 1966-67, and were being pushed to the periphery again by the army and the moderates in the Party and government in 1968.

Student Potential to Affect Future Policy. Several factors make it unlikely that student interests will be as peripheral to the political process as they were from 1950 to 1965. The memory of the Red Guards will linger on in the minds of bureaucrats, who probably will be somewhat more responsive to the demands of youth as a result. In addition, the youth have learned some lessons about voicing their interests which they are not likely to forget. Moreover, demographic trends probably will force the rulers to be particularly sensitive to the problems of youth. Their rapidly increasing numbers place an undeniable burden upon existing educational facilities and force the rulers to provide them with employment.

Further, the leaders will have to cope with the widespread cynicism, alienation, and anomie among students, a result of the broken promises of 1966 that idealistic and perhaps opportunistic students soon would be able to make important contributions to the pursuit of Mao's utopian vision. Only months after they made these promises, the leaders were coercing students to return to the same stations they had occupied prior to the Cultural Revolution. In the next few years, the idealistic appeals that worked in 1966 are unlikely to work again. The leaders probably will find that they can restore student confidence only by fulfilling specific demands for educational and employment opportunities.[43]

In addition, the problem of unequal educational opportunities for youth will certainly persist in the coming decades. According to an estimate by the American demographer John Aird, to achieve universal

secondary education by 1985, the secondary educational system would
have to enroll a minimum of six million additional students per year,
a virtually impossible rate of expansion. [44] In view of their deep commitment to building an egalitarian society, the rulers will probably again
feel called upon, as they were during the Cultural Revolution, to allev-
iate the tensions that develop as some youths enjoy upward mobility
while others return to the countryside.

As a result of these factors, one aspect of the Cultural Revolution, its emphasis upon the problems of youth, may foreshadow future
Chinese politics. In this sense, the Cultural Revolution may have sig-
nalled a partial return of youth to the political postion they held prior
to communist rule.

Party and Government Bureaucrats

Prior to the Cultural Revolution, the Chinese Communists described the organizational trinity that ran their country as the Party,
the government, and the army (tang, cheng, chun). But in February,
1967, when Mao and his entourage called for the formation of "Three-
Way Alliance" organizations in the provinces and cities, they referred
to a new trinity: 1) the Party and the government; 2)the army; and 3)the
revolutionary mass organizations. Although the Party and the government retained their separate identity, the delineation between them,
which had been so carefully preserved in theory prior to 1966, was
blurred.

The lumping together of Party and government in the Three Way
Alliance merely gave explicit acknowledgment to a development which
students of Chinese politics had long recognized. The overlapping membership in the two organizations, the existence of Party organizations
within the government, and the close supervision by the Party of government activities made it difficult to distinguish between the two.

Mao's placement of Party and government in the same category
in February, 1967 was the logical outcome of the intense Party involvement in governmental affairs which began during the Great Leap. In
oversimplified terms, the First Five Year Plan (1953-57) was run by
people in the governmental apparatus; the burden of economic development fell upon their shoulders. The Party remained a vanguard organization; members of the Party apparatus exercised broad control over
the government but remained aloof from day-to-day details, in order to
preserve their organizational and ideological purity. By 1957 however,

the officials in the governmental apparatus had become enmeshed in the society they were trying to change. Mao was alarmed by the alacrity with which government officials were increasingly bureaucratized from 1953 to 1957. So, in the Great Leap of 1958-60, he committed his vanguard organization, the CCP, directly to the battle to modernize China. But by 1965, many members of the CCP also had lost their reformist zeal. Inextricably intertwined with the entire society, the Party had come to contain within it all the contradictions, particularist loyalties, and tensions of Chinese society at large. In a sense, by 1966, Mao had used up two organizations in the pursuit of his vision.

In essence, the Cultural Revolution was an attempt by Mao and his associates to remove those government and Party cadres whom he perceived to be ineffective and to draw upon a fresh organization -- the PLA -- in the modernization effort. But such a design obviously did not coincide with the interests of the Party and government cadres, who wished to retain their jobs and protect the power of their organizations. (The reaction of the military officers, many of whom also opposed Mao's plans, is discussed below.) By the beginning of 1968, it appeared that most bureaucrats, with the exception of those at the top echelons on each level, had successfully resisted efforts to dislodge them. As a group, the Party and government bureaucrats retained their positions of power.

Bureaucratic Power and Vulnerabilities. What explains the ability of the bureaucrats to withstand the attacks upon their positions? Three obvious factors stand out. The performance of the routine tasks required for society to survive, from preventing epidemics to the merchandising of goods, depended upon the bureaucrats. To attempt to remove them, as nearly happened in Shanghai in early 1967, would result in the total disruption of society. In addition, the network of organizations developed under communist rule helped to unify the country. As Mao discovered in 1967, a concerted effort to destroy these organizations brought China to the precipice of civil war. Finally, in contrast to other aggregates in Chinese society, such as the peasants, the industrial workers and managers, and the intellectuals, the bureaucrats had their own organizations and enjoyed direct access to the policy formulation process. They were thus better equipped to defend their interests.

While these considerations help to explain why the bureaucrats as an aggregate remained in power, they do not explain the power of individual bureaucrats. Many individuals were able to build positions of considerable strength through their skilled use of personal ties, the manipulation of channels of communication, and the wise allocation of the resources at their disposal. Moreover, the opportunity to act in their own interest was increased by the discretion they enjoyed in making decisions, a discretion that arose in part from the vaguely worded directives they received from Peking.

Several factors made the individual Party or government bureaucrat vulnerable to outside control, particularly his dependence upon superiors to provide money and materials and to grant him promotions. Since these have been explored in the existing literature on contemporary Chinese politics, they need not be discussed here. [45] But in addition to the commonly mentioned techniques for maintaining discipline within the bureaucracy, two others deserve comment because of their prominence in the Cultural Revolution. First, the thorough files (tang-an) detailing their behavior over extended periods of time made individual bureaucrats vulnerable to innumerable distorted charges, all allegedly based on the record. Second, perhaps to an extent previously underestimated in earlier studies, the leaders of China have based their legitimacy upon the ideas and symbol of Mao Tse-tung. The denial of that symbol to an individual bureaucrat made it impossible for him to justify his role.

A word of caution is in order before we examine the sources of bureaucratic power and vulnerability in greater detail. The examples cited in the discussion below come from the indictments of top-level officials. Not all bureaucrats had the opportunity to engage in such activities. Nonetheless, the themes probably are applicable to the practices of lower-level officials, such as bureau chiefs and commune directors. A striking aspect of the purge documents is that they tend to confirm the picture of bureaucratic politics on the mainland obtained from former lower-level cadres interviewed in Hong Kong.

Personal Ties. Development of a network of reliable friends and loyal subordinates was a crucial part of building an invulnerable position. The purge of Li Ching-ch'uan, for example, revealed how this leader in China's Southwest apparently had built an apparatus loyal to him. He was accused of getting "hold of a number of lackeys and scattering them throughout the Southwest."[46] Prime examples cited were the appointment of his long-time colleagues Yen Hung-yen and Chia Chi-yun to the positions of First Secretary of Yunnan and Kweichow, respectively. Li apparently also was quick to remove subordinates who displayed disloyalty to him. More interesting, he appeared willing to employ and perhaps protect officials who were under a political cloud in Peking. He was accused of "taking in traitors and renegades and placing them in very important positions in the Southwest. "[47] (P'eng Teh-huai was the most noteworthy example, having obtained a position in the CCP Control Commission in the Southwest Bureau.) Finally, Li was careful to retain his contacts in Peking. Circumstantial evidence suggests that Li and the Southwest Bureau maintained a staff office in Peking to provide information on central politics and to lobby for the Southwest's interests. [48] The denunciations of Li also suggest that he maintained warm relations with several former associates, particularly Politburo members Ho Lung and Teng Hsiao-p'ing, after they moved to Peking.

T'ao Chu's proteges were mentioned by name. For example, T'ao was said to have promoted his disciple Wen Min-sheng, the deposed Governor of Honan, seven times in fourteen years, and "Wen showed his gratitude by lauding T'ao Chu to the sky. "[49] In fact, one of the clearest indications of the development of cliques came with T'ao Chu's rise to national prominence in the summer of 1966. Following him to Peking were three first secretaries in the Central-South: Wang Jen-chung of Hopeh, Chang P'ing-hua of Hunan, and Yao Wen-t'ao of Canton. When T'ao fell in late December, 1966, all three officials fell with him.

Control of Communication Channels. Another source of power, closely related to personal ties, was control over the channels of information. To establish extensive control over the communication network that extended beyond one's organization required the assistance of loyal subordinates and friends outside one's agency. Again, the purge of Li Ching-ch'uan provided some fascinating details of how a high level bureaucrat sought to seal his area and control the data that flowed from it. One charge against Li claimed:

> He never sent proper reports to the Party
> Central Committee and Chairman Mao, but
> rather sent in false reports. [50]

As an example of Li's behavior, Radio Chengtu described Li's alleged attempt in 1962 to portray Szechuan as in the grip of a spring drought that would seriously affect agricultural production. The broadcast continued:

> The old Szechuan Daily printed a report entitled
> 'Welcome Rain Falls Throughout the Province.' Li
> Ching-ch'uan, who was at a conference in Peking at
> this time, then rushed to telephone Szechuan to vig-

orously criticize this and forbid its publication.
After 1962, the press and radio in Szechuan were
instructed that they could only say "increase of
production," not "bumper harvest" or still less,
"great bumper harvest." The rate of production
increase for units of county level and above was
not to be reported. Thus, Li deliberately sealed
off news from Chairman Mao. [51]

Naturally, Mao was one of the key targets in the manipulation of
information. One reasonable hypothesis about Chinese politics is that
a crucial part of the game centers on attempts to control what Mao reads.
This hypothesis is supported by yet another charge against Li:

In 1966, just when the black gang element Peng
Chen was organizing his 'February Report Outline,'
he came specially to Szechuan with a handful of con-
federates to hold secret talks with Li Ching-chuan.
After returning to Peking, Peng telephoned Li to tell
him: 'Chairman Mao is reading the local (i. e., provincial as opposed to national - M. O.)papers every
day.' Peng urged Li to have more repudiation articles printed in the Szechuan papers... [52]

The list of techniques employed by ingenious officials to control
the flow of communications from their organizations is a long one. The
ones cited above -- falsifying statistics, suppressing weather reports,
and editing the news in anticipation of Mao's desires -- merely scratch
the surface. Escorting visiting officials to model, Potemkin-type areas,
tapping telephones, and enforcing strict censorship apparently were other
favorite techniques. The low turnover rate among local officials, particularly at the provincial level, often enabled a bureaucrat to develop
an extensive web of personal contacts and to establish effective control
over the flow of communications out of his unit. Though firm evidence
is hard to obtain, the scattered examples gain credibility because of
their strong resemblance to the way bureaucrats operated in traditional
China.

Control of Resources. Another source of a bureaucrat's power
was his control over material resources, which he often used to enhance
hi position. The charges against T'ao Chu, though perhaps exaggerated,
illustrate the practice:

The foundation of industry in Kwantung, especially light industry, is comparatively good.
If we resolutely implement Chairman Mao's in-
struction to make use of the original industry,
then we can do a better job in supporting industry
in the interior of China. However the counter-
revolutionary T'ao Chu stubbornly resisted and
opposed Chairman Mao's instructions... T'ao
said: 'We should build a complete industrial
system in Canton.'

In order to achieve this 'industrial system,' T'ao
did not actively help, make use of, reform, and
develop the original enterprises, especially in
small and poorly equipped street industry and handicraft enterprises. He held that this kind of industry was backward and could not be developed further
....He blindly chased after 'big' 'foreign,' and
'new,' trying his best to demand capital and equipment from the Center... [53]

Similar charges of increasing the wealth of his area at the expense of the center were made against Liu Chien-hsun, the former
First Secretary of Honan, who emerged unscathed in 1968 as head of
Honan's provincial revolutionary committee. [54] In violation of instructions from Peking, Liu allegedly encouraged peasants to plant peanuts
for sale to the state by promising them that in addition to the cash pay-
ments for each chin of marketed peanuts, the state would sell them one
chin and two ounces of reasonably priced grain. Under this incentive
system, Liu apparently hoped that the provincial warehouses would be
filled with more peanuts, a valuable commodity producing vegetable oil.
But his policy also caused a decrease in Honan's grain production, since
peanuts were grown on land that otherwise would have been planted in
grain. As a result, Honan, a grain-deficient province at the time, increased its dependence upon grain allotments from the center. In the
five years Liu worked in Honan (1961-66), the province allegedly received over six billion chin of grain shipped by the Central Committee.
The saying in Honan supposedly was: "Eat in Kwangtung and burn coal
from Shansi." When the Central Committee directed Liu to abolish his
program of guaranteed state sale of grain in exchange for marketed peanuts, he proved reluctant to comply.

Discretion in Policy Formulation. As these examples indicate--
and many similar instances can be cited-- the head of a unit often wished

to enhance the ability of his unit to bargain effectively with competing units. In many instances, moreover, he was able to succeed because of the wide discretion he enjoyed in formulating policy. The discretion was not as much the result of deliberate decentralization as it was the result of the vaguely worded directives he received.

This aspect of the environment in which Chinese bureaucrats worked needs to be placed in broader perspective. The information obtained during 1966-67 indicates that at least since the Tenth Plenum of 1962, the Central Committee of the CCP was deeply divided over a large number of issues. The disunified elite were unable to provide decisive, bold leadership to the bureaucracy. The divisions among the rulers were smoothed over through the issuance of vague directives. Often these were drafted by erstwhile colleagues of Mao such as Liu Shao-ch'i and P'eng Chen, who based their directives upon Mao's even more vague oral instructions. Examples are several important directives on rural policy issued during the 1960's, which have recently become available. What characterizes all of them is their ambiguity and sterility. [55] Instead of issuing explicit written orders, the top leaders apparently preferred to shape policy through a series of personal ad hoc conferences and trips to the provinces. The denunciations of Liu, Teng, and P'eng, for instance, indicated that these officials made frequent appearances in the provinces to inspect conditions, discuss problems, and deliver instructions. However, it seems that such conferences and appearances usually did not produce more precise directives.

This situation yielded both advantages and disadvantages to the bureaucrat. On the one hand, he was able to interpret the instructions in the light most favorable to his unit. Such behavior should not necessarily be viewed cynically, for most bureaucrats probably considered themselves loyal to Chairman Mao and the Party center, and had come to believe sincerely that the interests of their units coincided with the national interest. Yet, while the bureaucrat inevitably tended to bend the vague directives to suit his interests, thereby strengthening his unit, at the same time he was vulnerable to the accusation of deliberately misinterpreting the directives. Moreover, the higher level leaders who drafted the vague directives were open to the charges that they had violated the spirit of Mao's oral statements.

The conduct of the Four Clearances campaign in China's countryside in 1963-65 provided an excellent example. [56] In late 1962, Mao expressed dissatisfaction with the caliber and honesty of rural, basic-level cadres. However, while calling for a "Four Clearance" campaign to improve the situation, he did not address himself to the problem of standards. Instead, he handed the problem to Liu Shao-ch'i. In 1967, Mao claimed that Liu had violated his instructions by setting too high standards. Mao accused Liu of wishing to purge an excessive number of basic-level cadres, making them scapegoats for peasant discontent that should have been directed toward Liu. Despite Mao's claims, Liu's directives appear to have been so vague that no standard was clearly stated. The responses to Liu's directive were not uniform. Some provincial officials did not push the campaign, and during the Cultural Revolution they were accused of ignoring the problems of cadre corruption and the spread of capitalism. Other officials placed heavy emphasis upon Four Clearances, and in 1966-67, they were accused of unjustly condemning local cadres, thereby protecting Liu Shao-ch'i. In sum, the vagueness of the directives meant that when accused of anti-Maoist activity, a bureaucrat was unable to prove that he had not violated them.

The Dossier. Another source of a bureaucrat's vulnerability was the thorough dossier of his past activities. Rare was the Chinese bureaucrat who, at some point in his career, had not engaged in some form of conspicuous consumption, had not spoken somewhat disparagingly about the political system, had not barked orders to a subordinate rather than employing mass line techniques, or had not associated with "bad elements." Such activities often were recorded in his dossier, and were there to be used against him if the need arose. Subordinates who disliked their superior but were unable to damage him in any other way could fill their superior's files with charges of misconduct. Also in the dossier were remarks made during periods in which CCP policy was moderate. One such period occurred in 1961-62, when most leaders -- again including Mao--stressed the need of restoring the economy through material incentives. But such speeches appeared damning if reproduced out of context in 1966-67, when Mao stressed class struggle and the evils of material incentives.

As the purge swept the bureaucracy, contending factions tried to obtain the dossiers of their rivals in order to gather "black materials" on them. Not surprisingly, during the Cultural Revolution, there were constant reports of illegal seizures of personnel files, and repeated efforts were made to re-establish central control over them. A bureaucrat rightfully feared that his dossier contained enough evidence to condemn him, if it fell into malicious hands. The dossier made the bureaucrat vulnerable to the control of the man who held it.

Bureaucratic Claim to Legitimacy. Another source of bureaucratic vulnerability stemmed from the nature of the regime's claim to legitimacy. Although in the 1950's China's leaders justified their right to rule by nationalistic and economic appeals, through time they have increasingly based the claims of their legitimacy upon the sanctity of the thought of Mao Tse-tung. Thus, the authority of the bureaucrats was justified neither because their commands made the average Chinese more prosperous nor because their actions built a better China, but because their rule was in accordance with the thought of Mao Tse-tung. The powerholders in China had equated the right of rule with being a disciple of Mao Tse-tung. Whoever manipulated the symbol of Mao-- and when Mao was vigorous, he manipulated it-- controlled the bureaucrat's claim to legitimacy.

Once an individual bureaucrat's loyalty to Mao was questioned and his dossier was made public, his power--based upon his network of friends, his control over information, and the allocation of his limited resources--gradually eroded. Other bureaucrats sought to disassociate themselves from him, for fear that they might be labelled part of his gang. He became a target for and suffered the humiliation of struggle. He was isolated.

Strategy for Survival. Working under the intense physical and psychological pressure of the Cultural Revolution and realizing his vulnerability to purge, the individual bureaucrat had political survival as his main objective. The strategies he employed were to cling tenaciously to the source of his legitimacy by claiming that he was a good Maoist, to seal his unit off from outside interference, as much as possible, and to secure the continued support of his loyal subordinates. These tactics were not sufficient to protect all officials, but, given their crucial social role, most Party and government bureaucrats weathered the storm and remained in positions of power as the Cultural Revolution subsided in early 1968.

Military

To appreciate the power and influence of the military in Chinese society, one must understand the position of the PLA during the Cultural Revolution. While most analysts agree that the PLA played a crucial role in 1966-67, they differ in their evaluations.

The PLA Rise to Power. Some analysts stated that the military had taken over. Impressive evidence exists to support this contention. PLA units were dispatched to factories and schools, where the troop commanders assumed important leadership functions. The PLA, already deeply immersed in such tasks as running the railroads and organizing propaganda prior to the Cultural Revolution, increased its responsibilities in these vital areas. When one looked at the top official in each of the provinces, one found that although a few of the new and surviving officials had careers within the CCP, most were former military officers. Some of them, such as Li Yuan in Hunan or Li Ts'ai-han in Kweichow, had risen from obscurity; their names were not listed in the standard biographic guides to China's leaders. In Peking, the national holidays were presided over by military men. Newspaper editorials throughout 1967 stressed the crucial role performed by the PLA in society. In 1967, Mao's closest comrade-in-arms and his likely successor was said to be the Minister of Defense and head of the Military Affairs Committee, Lin Piao. The nationally debated issues reflected the concerns of the military apparatus: the amount of time the army should spend in physical training versus the amount of time spent on the study of Mao's works, the role of the PLA troops stationed in factories and schools, the relations between the military and other sectors of society, the obligations of the regional garrison commanders to obey the center, and even the role of the navy in domestic peace keeping functions. When the leaders of the country are drawn from the military, when the issues debated in the press are of particular relevance to the military, and when the military stationed its troops in non-military units throughout the country, the evidence strongly suggests that a military takeover occurred.

Moreover, there were signs that the rise of the PLA was the result of a conscious rivalry with the CCP. The PLA had intimate organizational links with the Red Guards, who led the attacks upon the CCP apparatus. One of the key Red Guard units, for example, came from the Peking Aviation Institute, a school with close PLA connections. Some Red Guard newspapers also spoke of an organizational rivalry between the Party and the PLA. For instance, the Ministry of Railways and the PLA shared jurisdiction over the railways. The Minister of Railways, Lu Cheng-ts'ao, was accused of wanting to control the armed railroad personnel, who were under PLA command. Lu allegedly maintained:

> The Public Security Ministry controls its own
> public security forces. Why shouldn't the Railway
> Ministry control railway forces? [57]

Lu was accused of "wanting to usurp the power and authority of the PLA."

Invective in a similar vein had been directed earlier against Teng T'o, the dismissed editor of Peking Daily:

> We must warn Teng T'o and his ilk that the right to 'contend' is not allowed in the PLA, and the fighters of the people will wipe out those who dare to stick their nose into the army under the pretext of contention. [58]

These quotes hinting at a possible PLA-CCP rivalry lend weight to an interpretation of the Cultural Revolution that stresses a PLA takeover from the Party.

On the other hand, several factors made it misleading simply to state that the military seized power in China. First, the military apparatus in China lacked clear cut organizational identity and was thoroughly interwoven with the CCP. The commanders of the PLA who acquired power in 1967 probably were also CCP members. The rise to power of PLA commanders can be seen as a shift in the balance of power within the Party, with CCP members serving in the military sector taking power from those in charge of such internal Party work as organization and propaganda.

Second, not all elements in the military enhanced their position in 1966-67. In fact, many leaders of the PLA were purged. The most noteworthy cases included the dismissals of Chief-of-Staff Lo Jui-ch'ing, the head of the Political Department, Hsiao Hua, and Marshal Ho Lung, but the purge extended to garrison commanders, department heads, political commissars, and others. [59] If one is to speak in organizational terms, one cannot speak of a PLA takeover; one must speak of the seizure of power by specific units within the PLA. But here, no discernable pattern emerges, although there are some tantalizing hints. For instance, in recent years three newly appointed regional commanders came from the Shenyang garrison command, [60] Kiangsi province was occupied during the Cultural Revolution by troops dispatched from the Tsinan garrison command, [61] and the Wuhan rebellion was quelled, in part, through the dispatch from Shanghai of a naval force attached to the East China fleet. [62] A hypothesis that merits testing is that several army, navy, and air commands (such as Shenyang and Tsinan), perhaps owing allegiance to Lin Piao, acted together, that forces from these units occupied various areas, and that the newly risen military personnel were drawn primarily from these units. But until firm evidence in uncovered, such hypotheses must be held in abeyance. Thus, the unqualified assertion that the PLA had risen to power glosses over the difficult yet crucial problem of a complex process within the PLA which led to the promotion of some and the purge of other military figures.

A third reason that the image of a "military takeover" needs qualification was its incompleteness. Many government and Party officials, even at higher levels, survived. Hunan provides a convenient example. Li Yuan and PLA unit 6900, which had been garrisoned in Hengyang, began to dominate news items from Ch'angsha. But Li appears to be the leader of a group that includes Hua Kuo-feng and Chang Po-sen, both of whom have long records of leadership in Party and government affairs in Hunan. Hua was First Secretary of Hsiang-t'an Special District in Hunan in the early 1950's, served as head of the provincial government's Culture and Education Office and the Party's United Front Department in the late 1950's, and was an active Party secretary and Vice Governor in the early 1960's. Chang's tenure in Hunan also dates back to the early 1950's, when he was head of the Provincial Party Finance and Trade Department. The Hunan pattern was observable elsewhere. Leaders of the PLA won positions of power, but their rise was not accompanied by the total removal of leading government and Party bureaucrats.

A fourth consideration against labelling the enhanced power of the military as a "takeover" was the noticeable reluctance of some military leaders to assume their new roles in domestic affairs. Military commanders in China were concerned with the capacity of their forces to fight against foreign powers. As the PLA became increasingly involved with domestic functions in the 1960's, of necessity it sacrificed some of its capacity to wage war. Lo Jui-ch'ing apparently was one of the officials opposed to the policy. Moreover, since the PLA automatically created enemies when it tried to restore order between conflicting groups and individuals, local commanders were reluctant to become involved. If the PLA intervened on the side of one Red Guard organization, the other side became disenchanted. If the PLA tried to work out compromises, then the organizations accused the PLA of not settling the dispute on the basis of principles. During the early part of 1967, many PLA commanders apparently tried to shield their units from the turmoil, but the spreading chaos could be dampened only through military intervention. To a certain extent, it was less that the PLA eagerly seized power than that it reluctantly filled an organizational vacuum.

Sources of PLA Power. Even with these qualifications, it remains true that the PLA significantly increased its power and influence. Part of the explanation for this rests in Mao's confidence in Lin Piao

and the PLA, a confidence inspired by the political program carried
out in the army from 1959 to 1965. Because the PLA stood apart from
civilian society, ideological indoctrination probably could be carried
out more effectively in the PLA than in other institutions in society.
The effectiveness of the program in the PLA led Mao, who perhaps
failed to discern the inherent differences between military and non-military organizations, to display impatience with the comparatively inef-
ficient indoctrination efforts undertaken by the Party propagandists in
civilian society, and to replace them with PLA personnel.

Another factor involved in the rise of the military was a personnel
policy which enabled it to retain its vigor and extend its influence. Whereas other organizations in Chinese society frequently lacked institutionalized retirement processes, had aged leaders, and suffered from clogged
channels of upward mobility, the PLA was able to transfer its older and
less competent members to non-military organizations. Not only did
the transfer of veterans to positions in government, Party, and industry
enable the PLA to solve its own internal problems of mobility and retirement, but it also meant that the PLA saturated the non-military organizations with men whose loyalties may in part have belonged to the military.

A further reason for the rise of the PLA was the increased importance of the foreign and domestic functions it performs. In foreign
affairs, the leaders of China believed themselves to be encircled by
hostile powers. They give primacy to the acquisition of a nuclear capability. In the tense situation of the mid-1960's in East Asia, with problems of national defense a prime concern, it was perhaps natural that
military men came to play a more vital role in national politics.

Domestically, although firm documentation is lacking, it appears
that the rulers increasingly had to rely on coercive means to control the
population. As their ability to elicit a mass response through idealistic
appeals diminished and their initial wide-spread support waned, the
leaders administered a more harsh criminal law. With the population
growth and the possibly growing gap between urban and rural living
standards, the rulers had to exercise increasingly stringent control over
population movements. In 1966-67, the situation became acute, and force
of arms became a major way of restoring law and order. Those who
wielded the instruments of coercion, people associated with the PLA
and the public security forces, rose to power as the demand for their
skills increased.

Yet another source of military power was its control of rail, air, and major river transport, giving its members and their allies a mobility which people in other organizations lacked. During the rapidly evolving political situation in 1966-67, access to air transport proved especially important. Chou En-lai, for example, was able at several crucial junctures to fly to trouble spots to negotiate or mediate disputes. In other instances, key groups were flown to Peking. One day after the May 6th incident in Chengtu, for instance, several of those involved were already in Peking to discuss the Szechuan situation with Chou, Ch'en Po-ta, K'ang Sheng, and Chiang Ch'ing. Further, to communicate their message to the peasants, perhaps indicating an inability to use a recalcitrant propaganda apparatus, the leadership airdropped leaflets to peasants in Kwangsi and Hupeh province in the spring. [63]

An additional reason for the enhanced power of military personnel may have been their relative self-sufficiency. In contrast to members of other hierarchies, their organization produced a considerable portion of the goods they consumed. Moreover, the PLA had an important role in directing the machine-building industries, the mining and extractive industries, and the agricultural reclamation projects in China's border provinces. When production and delivery schedules fell behind, as happened in early 1967, the army may have been in a better position to sustain itself. (This observation, however, is a logical inference rather than an adequately documented conclusion.)

In sum, the principal reasons for the rise of the PLA were similar to those for the increased importance of the military in many of the economically developing countries. [64] It won the confidence of the national leader. It stood somewhat isolated from society, thereby retaining a vigor and élan which the CCP inevitably lost when it became so involved in societal affairs that its parts came to represent particular interests. The post-service affiliations of former military personnel enabled the PLA to extend its influence to other organizations. Its control of resources enabled it to have an independent base of power. Because the PLA and the public security forces were the coercive agents of the ruler, these organizations came to the fore as the maintenance of the state increasingly rested upon coercion. Moreover, since the reasons for their rise are likely to persist, military personnel seem destined to be at the center of Chinese politics for the forseeable future.

Conclusion

The power and influence of the major occupational groupings in Chinese society, as revealed in the Cultural Revolution, can now be briefly summarized. The peasants influenced policy indirectly; their interests were voiced by sympathetic government and Party bureaucrats and the military leaders. The top policy formulators tried to anticipate peasant reactions primarily because of their economic importance.

In one of the significant aspects of the Cultural Revolution, the industrial managers and the industrial workers displayed their power to act swiftly and to affect policies ruinous to their interests. Members of these occupational groups appear to be acquiring increased power as China industrializes.

Intellectuals, increasingly differentiated in the roles they perform, differed in their ability to alter policy affecting them. Social critics were totally vulnerable to control, and teachers were shown basically to serve at the pleasure of the ruler. Scientific and technical personnel, however, saw their interests taken into account, particularly if they were engaged in research that gained them firm supporters among the military.

The students demonstrated that, when allied with elements of the bureaucracy and the military, they could become a powerful force, but that without allies, they were unable to remain a politically dominant group. Nonetheless, a study of youth suggests that their problems demand urgent attention, and for this reason their demands probably will elicit a continued response from those at the center of power.

Though many government and Party bureaucrats were purged, they displayed their ability to survive as an occupational group at the center of power. Their functions proved vital; moreover, they had learned some of the tactics necessary to defend their interests.

Finally, members of the military apparatus moved to the very center of power during the Cultural Revolution. An analysis of the sources of their power and influence indicates that their importance will persist.

This summary, however, has several limitations which should be made explicit. The occupational groups analyzed are broadly defined; in reality, each category includes many kinds of positions. For example, instead of analyzing Party and government bureaucrats as one group, a more rigorous analysis would examine the interests and power of the bureaucrats in the various functional systems into which the Party and government were divided; finance and trade, agriculture, forestry, and water conservancy, industry and communications, culture and education, law enforcement, and so on. A more rigorous analysis of industrial workers would distinguish among skilled and unskilled workers in large, medium, and small factories. Their attitudes and ability to affect public policy were probably different.

In addition, this paper's exclusive focus upon occupational groups neglects other important ways of subdividing the population, such as into geographical, attitudinal, ethnic, or class groups. Indeed, one would gain considerable insight into Chinese politics by asking the question: What does the Cultural Revolution tell us about the relative power and influence of people in different geographic areas in China? Moreover, there is considerable evidence that conflict within the occupational groups was often based upon class and status groups. Among students, apparently, conflict sometimes broke out between children of cadres and children from less favored backgrounds. (The important United Action Red Guards, for instance, reportedly drew its strength from the children of cadres.) The conflict between the permanent and temporary workers was a struggle between two classes. Conflict between bureaucrats often involved disputes between high-ranking and low-ranking cadres. The pro-Maoist leaders apparently tended to draw strong support from the lower classes and status groups, a facet of the Cultural Revolution that does not become clear if one focuses solely upon occupational groups.

Moreover, the Cultural Revolution provides a narrow and unusual time span from which to view the interests and power of occupational groups. They were able to act upon their interests, in part, because of the diminished capacity of the elite to provide effective leadership. (One reason for their reduced capacity, however, was the increased ability of occupational groups to defend their interests. The two phenomena were inter-related.) If the rulers recapture their former strength, or if they resort to different techniques in order to elicit a response (for example, an increased use of material incentives), then the interests and abilities of various groups to affect policy will change.

Finally, another limitation of the exclusive focus upon group interests and power is its neglect of other important subjects, such as the role of ideas. A satisfactory explanation for the persistence of radical thought in China, so crucial for an understanding of the Cultural

Revolution, must go beyond an analysis of student radicalism and the interests of occupational groups, for the radicals were found among all of them. [65] Ultimately, for a thorough understanding of Chinese politics one must integrate group analysis with an analysis of the leaders and the culture and ideas that move them.

In spite of these limitations, however, occupational group analysis enables one to approach China from a fresh vantage point. Transitory factors affecting Chinese politics, such as the power of a particular individual, factional rivalries, or a war on China's border, are blotted out in order to highlight more permanent developments. A clearer picture emerges of the occupational groups that will exercise the greatest demands upon the top leaders, no matter who those leaders might be.

This study suggests that in the years ahead, China's leaders will confront several occupational groups that will effectively articulate their interests: the military personnel, the government and Party bureaucrats, and increasingly, the industrial managers and workers. Moreover, the leaders will have to pay urgent attention to the problems of students, and respond to the demands of scientists and technicians. They will face considerable constraints in formulating their policies toward the peasants. It is highly likely that Chinese politics is moving into an era marked by intense bargaining between a weakened central leadership, its authority seriously eroded during the Cultural Revolution, and powerful occupational groups. The leaders will not be in an enviable position, as they attempt to reconcile and mediate the conflicting demands made by these groups.

40

Footnotes

1. Barrington Moore, Terror and Progress USSR: Some Sources of Change and Stability in the Soviet Dictatorship, Harvard University Press, 1954, and Isaac Deutscher, Russia: What Next, Oxford University Press, 1953.

2. Barrington Moore, Social Origins of Dictatorship and Democracy, Beacon Press, 1966.

3. For an analysis stressing this approach, see Philip Bridgham, "Mao's Cultural Revolution," China Quarterly, No. 29, January-March 1967, p. 1-35.

4. Analyses stressing this approach include: Franz Schurmann, "The Attack of the Cultural Revolution on Ideology and Organization," in Tang Tsou and P'ing-ti Ho, ed., China's Heritage and the Communist Political System, University of Chicago Press, 1968 forthcoming, and Chalmers Johnson, "China: The Cultural Revolution in Structural Perspective," Asian Survey, Vol. VIII, No. 1, January 1968, p. 1-15.

5. Analyses stressing this approach include: John W. Lewis, "The Leaders and the Commissar: The Chinese Political System in the Last Days of the Revolution," in Tang Tsou and P'ing-ti Ho, ed., China's Heritage, op. cit.; and Richard Baum, "Ideology Redivivus," Problems of Communism, May-June 1967, p. 1-11.

6. An analysis stressing this approach is Richard Solomon, "Communication Patterns and the Chinese Revolution," a paper delivered to the annual meeting of the American Political Science Association, September 1967.

7. Radio Kweiyang, June 28, 1967.

8. J. Chester Cheng, ed., The Politics of the Chinese Red Army, Hoover Institution, 1966. See p. 12-19 for example.

9. See Peking Review, No. 35, August 25, 1967, pp. 6-7 and No. 36, September 1, 1967, p. 14; Tokyo Mainichi, August 22, 1967.

10. See China News Analysis, No. 645 and 647. For a dramatic account of one such uprising, see Joint Publications Research Service (henceforth JPRS) 44,052, January 17, 1968, p. 16-23.

11. China Topics, YB 415, February 23, 1967, part III.

12. See especially Eric Wolf, Peasants, Prentice Hall, 1966 , p. 91; and Mehmet Bequirj, Peasantry in Revolution, Cornell, 1966 , p. 14-15.

13. For summary discussions of the role of agriculture in the Chinese economy, see especially: Alexander Eckstein, Communist China's Economic Growth and Foreign Trade, McGraw-Hill, 1966, p. 47; Marion Larson, "China's Agriculture under Communism," in Joint Economic Committee of the United States Congress, Economic Profile of Mainland China, Government Printing Office, 1968, Vol. I. , esp. p. 205; and Feng-hua Mah, "Public Investment in Communist China," Journal of Asian Studies, Vol. XXI, No. 1, November 1961, p. 46.

14. China Topics, No. 415, February 23, 1967.

15. Crucial here was Chiang Ch'ing's speech of September 5, 1967. An excellent summary of this period is in Chalmers Johnson, "China: The Cultural Revolution in Structural Perspective," op. cit. , p. 10-15.

16. John R. Wenmohs, "Agriculture in Mainland China - 1967," Current Scene, Vol. V, No. 21, December 15, 1967.

17. As a start, however, see: Evelyn Anderson, "Shanghai Upheaval," Problems of Communism, January-February, 1968, p. 12-22; "Sources of Labor Discontent in China: The Worker Peasant System," Current Scene, Vol. VI, No. 5, March 15, 1968 ; Andrew Watson, "Cultural Revolution in Sian," Far Eastern Economic Review, April 20, 1967, April 27, 1967, and May 4, 1967; and Neale Hunter, "The Cultural Revolution in Shanghai," Far Eastern Economic Review, June 1, 1967, June 22, 1967, and July 6, 1967.

18. "More on the Question of Grasping the Revolution Firmly and Stimulating Production," Jen-min Jih-pao (People's Daily, henceforth, JMJP), November 22, 1966, in Survey of the Chinese Mainland Press (henceforth SCMP), No. 3825, p. 1-4.

19. JPRS 40,274, p. 34.

20. For another analysis, see China News Analysis, No. 644.

21. Peking Review, No. 1, January 1, 1967, p. 12.

22. Radio Foochow, January 9, 1967.

23. SCMP, No. 3913, p.2.

24. For texts, see China Topics, No. 418, March 8, 1967.

25. SCMP, No. 3904, p. 9.

26. For more detailed chronology see China Quarterly, No. 30, p. 209, 232-233.

27. For a general discussion, see Edward Shils, "The Intellectuals in the Political Development of the New States," in John Kautsky, ed., Political Change in Underdeveloped Countries, John Wiley, 1962, p. 195-235.

28. For the editorials attacking Wu Han and the Three Family Village, see The Great Socialist Cultural Revolution in China, Peking: Foreign Language Press, 1966-67, 1-3. A collection of the satires attacking Mao, which appeared in the Peking Press in the early 1960's was reprinted in Taiwan: Teng T'o shih-wen hsuan-ch'i, Taipei: Freedom Press, 1966.

29. Peking Review, No.1, January 1, 1967, p. 15.

30. Peking Review, No.33, August 12, 1966, p. 10.

31. Seymour Lipset, ed., Student Politics, Berkeley: Institute of International Studies, 1966, p. 140.

32. Not all Red Guards were students, it should be noted, nor were all students Red Guards. Though in this section I discuss the student sector of Chinese Society with a particular focus upon the more radical students, my remarks may be applicable to Chinese youth in general.

33. See China Topics, No. 427, May 23, 1967, Section F; JPRS 41,514.

34. This point is stressed throughout in A. Doak Barnett and Ezra Vogel, Cadres, Bureaucracy, and Political Power in Communist China, Columbia University Press, 1967.

35. For one discussion of antagonistic student-teacher relations, see Radio Canton, Regional #2, April 3, 1967.

36. See James Townsend's excellent study, The Revolutionization of Chinese Youth, Berkeley: Center for Chinese Studies Monograph, 1966.

37. China Youth, No. 7, 1963, p. 11.

38. See Donald Munro, "Maxims and Realities in China's Educational Policy," Asian Survey, Vol. 7, No. 4, April, 1967, p. 254-272.

39. See Richard Solomon, The Chinese Revolution and the Politics of Dependency, MS., University of Michigan, 1966.

40. JPRS 41,313, June 8, 1967, p. 14-21.

41. Radio Shanghai, July 9, 1967.

42. This theme is suggested in Philip Bridgham, "Mao's Cultural Revolution," op. cit.

43. The argument is derived from G. William Skinner's theory of a compliance cycle in China. See his important, "Compliance and Leadership in Rural Communist China," a paper delivered to the 1965 Annual Meeting of the American Political Science Association.

44. John Aird, "Population Growth and Distribution in Mainland China," Joint Economic Committee of U.S. Congress, An Economic Profile of Mainland China, Vol. II, p. 341-403.

45. In particular, see Audrey Donnithorne, China's Economic System, Allen and Unwin, 1967, esp. last chapter, and Barnett and Vogel, Cadres, Bureaucracy..., op. cit.

46. Radio Kweiyang, June 4, 1967.

47. Ibid.

48. JPRS 42,349, August 25, 1967, p. 63; China Topics, No. 437, August 18, 1967, p. 9.

49. Radio Chengchow, October 12, 1967.

50. Radio Kweiyang, June 4, 1967; Radio Chengtu, October 26, 1967.

51. Radio Chengtu, October 13, 1967.

52. Radio Chengtu, September 5, 1967.

53. Radio Canton, December 1, 1967.

54. JPRS 43,357, November 16, 1967, p. 29-30.

55. The Hoover Institution has a complete file of these directives obtained from GRC authorities in Taiwan.

56. For discussion of "Four Clearances," see Charles Neuhauser, "The Chinese Communist Party in the 1960's," China Quarterly, No. 32. Also, Richard Baum and Frederic Teiwes, Ssu-Ch'ing: The Socialist Education Movement of 1962-1966, Berkeley: Center for Chinese Studies, 1968.

57. JPRS 41, 249, June 2, 1967, p. 46-67.

58. Radio Peking, May 24, 1966.

59. In China News Summary, No. 188-194.

60. Ibid.

61. Radio Nanchang, September 6, 1967 and October 9, 1967.

62. Radio Wuhan, October 22, 1967.

63. Radio Wuhan, March 8, 1967; Radio Nanning, February 28, 1967.

64. See, for example, Lucian Pye, "Armies in the Process of Political Development," in his Aspects of Political Development , Little Brown, 1966, p. 172-187.

65. For sensitive studies of some of the sources of radicalism, see Maurice Meisner, Li Ta-chao and the Origins of Chinese Marxism, Harvard University Press, 1967, and Olga Lang, Pa Chin and his Writings, Harvard University Press, 1967.

THE CHINESE ECONOMY IN 1967

Carl Riskin*

Introduction

Economists, forced to view the Chinese economy from afar, have often resembled the proverbial blind men describing an elephant. Moreover, as the elephant has grown, even less of it has been revealed until some have been tempted to cease groping altogether, invoking instead ideal conceptions of elephant nature as substitutes for unavailable facts.

At the current stage of the Cultural Revolution in particular, it is hazardous either to generalize broadly from the partial view available or to rely heavily on preconceptions as to which of the protagonists can count human nature an ally in the struggle. Certain facts are known about the Chinese economy over the past year, certain interpretations, sometimes contradictory, have been broached, and I will review the main examples of both in this paper. Some preliminary conclusions which emerge from such a review are set out briefly below, with the caveat that they are tentative. Subsequent sections then take up the situation in agriculture, industry, and foreign trade respectively in greater detail, and the paper concludes with some general observations on the economic issues involved in the Cultural Revolution.

Agriculture seems to have had a very good year in 1967. Disruptions stemming from the Cultural Revolution were concentrated around the spring planting process, the transportation of imported chemical fertilizers and other inputs to the countryside, and the marketing of grains. But these difficulties apparently were not sufficient, given good weather and an increase in local domestic supplies of inputs, to prevent a substantial increase in production of major foodgrains over that of 1966. Nevertheless much disagreement exists over the level of production in recent years, and the difference in estimates for 1967 is large enough to influence substantially one's diagnosis of the state of the

* I am indebted to the members of the "Communist China, The Year-in-Review" seminar, and in particular to Robert Dernberger, for penetrating criticisms of an earlier draft of this paper.

economy in general. Official reports also claim solid increases in output of major industrial crops. The economic effectiveness of a good crop depends of course on whether an adequate amount of it is marketed, and there are indications of marketing problems during the late summer and autumn, but their extent and significance are still unclear.

In industry, on the other hand, the extended preoccupation of workers and managers with the factional struggles stemming from the Cultural Revolution suggests that there was more substantial disruption of production. No overall statistics for gross value of industrial production or its increase in 1967 seem to be available. There is also a general paucity of progress reports for important industrial products, particularly within the heavy industry group. General claims of increased production have been made for a variety of light industrial products, however, as well as for agricultural machinery and tools.

China's foreign trade regained in 1966 its previous peak level of 1959 although its composition by trading partners has changed dramatically. The overall volume of trade in 1967 was probably substantially the same. However, exports fell while imports rose, so that the continuing trade surplus of recent years almost certainly dwindled, possibly becoming a deficit. Trade with China's most important partner, Japan, fell after a sharp increase in 1966, but it is not clear that the Cultural Revolution is to blame for this. The upward trend in trade with Western Europe, however, has continued through 1967. Latest available reports put the volume of wheat imports for fiscal 1966-1967 down from the previous fiscal year, and there is some indication of a further decrease in 1967-1968, although it is certainly too early to draw such a conclusion confidently.

That the economy has not been unaffected by the ebb and flow of the Cultural Revolution throughout the year is obvious. While it is impossible at this time to measure with any certainty the magnitude of this influence, the balance of evidence suggests that it has not been sufficient to preclude a rebound in industrial growth, providing a political situation conducive to stable working conditions is brought about.

Agriculture

Although there is general agreement on the limited proposition that 1967 saw very favorable weather conditions over most of China, nevertheless the gap between "official"[1] estimates and those developed at the U.S. Consulate in Hong Kong continues to widen; the highest estimate from China puts the size of the 1967 harvest at 230 million metric tons, one-fourth larger than the 187 million tons estimated by the U.S. Agricultural Attaché in Hong Kong.[2] Such a difference, which is of the order of magnitude of the entire marketed portion of the crop, must influence one's estimate of success or failure in China's development efforts over the last several years as well as one's prognosis for the future.

An assessment of last year's situation is complicated by the existence of a second, albeit tentative, claimant to the status of official estimate for foodgrain output. Hsieh Fu-chih is said to have reported on October 5, 1967,that "production of grain has increased by 18 billion to 21 billion catties over last year..." Some six weeks later, Chou En-lai reportedly announced that "the output of food crops this year has gone up by 5 - 6 percent..."[3] As one observer writes, "assuming that both estimates pertain to the same base, then we know that the Chinese estimated grain production in 1966 at about 179 million metric tons and that they expect production in 1967 to be about 188 million to 190 million tons."[4] Since the revised U.S. Consulate estimate for 1966 foodgrain output is 178 million M.T. and its 1967 estimate is 187 million M.T., this reasoning can be regarded as providing some support for the Consulate methods.

The extent of such support is more limited than is readily apparent, however. First, the Hsieh-Chou estimate is not as precise as the above reasoning implies, for there is no number of which 5 - 6 percent defines a range of 18 - 21 billion. Therefore, the sets of statistics do not imply a single estimate for 1966 of 179 million metric tons. Second, there is no particular reason for assuming that both men referred to the same estimated increase for 1967. Their speeches were reported to have occurred six weeks apart toward the end of the harvest, when measurement can be assumed to have been still in progress, so that the estimated increase may well have changed. The implied total output would be quite sensitive to such a change. For example, if the increased output were confirmed to be at the lower end of Hsieh Fu-chih's range, then Chou's percentages would imply an output of 150 - 180 million M.T. in 1966, whereas if it were confirmed to be at the upper end, the corresponding figure would be 175 - 210 million M.T. The range would thus be wide enough to provide support for any of the opinions extant on the state of Chinese agriculture and, therefore, for none.

In addition, of course, information conveyed to us by way of Red Guard and similar publications must be treated with caution. Even if the source is authentic, the accuracy of information contained therein depends upon the reliability of the reporter. In this particular case, Chou is reported to have made the erroneous statement that Burma and Thailand, among other countries, "which used to export food grains before now have to import them. "[5] If one regards the Premier as unlikely to have made such an error, then one must be equally cautious in evaluating the other factual statements in the report.

Finally, we have Anna Louise Strong's alternative figure for 1967--presumably based on government information--of 230 million tons, and a spate of government announcements characterizing the harvest last year as an "all-time record. " While a difference in estimates, representing different data-gathering techniques or construction methods, would be understandable under the circumstances, a difference implying that Peking deliberately keeps two sets of books would inject a new difficulty into the work of students of the Chinese economy, most of whom have rejected this change heretofore. [6]

The disparity between the Strong and Consulate estimates reflects generally different appraisals of the state of Chinese agriculture. The Chinese not only regard the 1967 harvest as an advance over a record figure for 1966, but also claim that "the rate of increase in production of China's foodgrains for the whole of 1967 will... greatly exceed the average annual rate of increase for the five years since 1962. "[7] The Consulate observers, however, regard 1964 as the record year and the 1966 harvest as substantially smaller. While agreeing that weather conditions in 1967 were "more favorable for farming than during any of the preceding 17 years of Communist Party control of mainland China, " they nevertheless maintain that the effects of the Cultural Revolution partly negated this positive influence so that the 1967 harvest probably "will fall slightly below the level of the record harvest of 1964. "[8]

Part of the difference in output estimates can be traced to varying interpretations of the effect of the Cultural Revolution on the production and supply of inputs and capital goods to agriculture. On this subject official claims are categorical. "This year 40 percent more chemical fertilizer is available, 30 percent more insecticide, and 20 percent more sprayers than last year. "[9] Reports for 17 provinces and regions were said to show bigger increases in 1967 in irrigated acreage, mechanized and electrified drainage, and irrigation facilities and pump-operated wells than in any other year since 1961; a considerable extension of terraced and raised fields and of acreage sown to improved seed strains was also reported. [10] In line with a continuing policy of industry

serving agriculture, production of farm machinery and tools was said
to have grown substantially in 1967 over 1966, with increases in output
ranging from 20 to 200 percent in such products as mechanized insecticide sprayers and dusters, gears, cement boats, flour milling machines, and cotton gins. Large increases were also registered in spare
parts and accessories for tractor engines and in metal and bamboo tools.[11]
Retail sales of chemical fertilizers, semi-mechanized farm implements,
insecticides, and plastic sheets for agricultural use increased over 1966.
Consistent with its claims of increased supplies, Peking announced price
reductions averaging something under 4 percent on agricultural producer
goods; prices of chemical fertilizers, insecticides, and small motors
and transformers seem to have accounted for the bulk of this reduction,
the first two falling 10 to 15 percent and the last 20 percent. Most of
the readjustment in prices involved reductions for industrial commodities
sold in remote areas so as to reduce regional price differentials. [12]

Another aspect of Chinese reports on inputs to agriculture concerns the results of a three-year campaign against wheat rust, centering
on the breeding and popularization of rust-resistant, high-yield strains
of seed as well as the development of chemical preventives. In 1964,
only 20 million mou of China's wheat area of some 400 million mou were
sown to the new seed. This area is said to have been doubled in 1965,
extended to 68 percent of the winter wheat fields in 1966, and presumably
further increased last year. [13] This may be a factor related to the claimed
superior performance of traditional grain-deficit provinces of the north
in 1967. [14] Another noteworthy communique reported the increasing use
of aircraft for crop dusting and spraying in Hunan, Honan, Hopei, Anhwei,
and Sinkiang. [15]

In contrast to this sanguine view of the flow of resources into
agriculture, some outside observers believe the Cultural Revolution
caused reductions in the supply of inputs from abroad, from industry,
and from the peasants themselves. There is no doubt that disruptions
occurred. The Hsinhua release celebrating the bumper harvest itself
stated that opponents of the Cultural Revolution, using among others the
method of "counter-revolutionary economism," attempted to subvert production during the early spring. [16] But how extensive and prolonged were
such disruptions?

Agriculture is generally thought to have been relatively immune
to the pressures of the Cultural Revolution during most of 1966. However, it was carried to the countryside in December, and until late
January left a record of some disorder. It is by no means clear what

the Red Guards in the rural villages actually did, but there is some evidence of pressure to reject suspect commune leadership as well as those institutions regarded ideologically as compromises, such as the self-retained plots and the free market. There are reports of peasant raids on grain storehouses and of illegal distribution of grain meant for collective reserves and even seed. It is impossible to know the extent of such actions, and even their significance is ambiguous in view of the debate which we now know took place over the degree of centralization of grain reserves. Mao's position seems to have favored greater peasant control over reserves compared to that of his opponents (See Section on Foreign Trade).

The general disorganization resulting from the introduction of a highly polemical and emotional atmosphere into the villages must also have caused a decline in work inputs at a time when the farmers are ordinarily building and repairing irrigation and drainage facilities, over-hauling machinery and equipment, and generally preparing for the spring planting. In some places they flocked to neighboring towns to participate in the battle. [17] The result of all this was an admittedly bad situation at the beginning of the year. In Kwangtung, for example, "this year's spring farm work started somewhat later than usual due to sabotage by the handful of capitalist-roaders."[18]

After the pressure was eased in late January and the central authorities began emphasizing the primacy of spring planting the situation improved, and from February on there does not seem to have been such serious direct interference by the Cultural Revolution in agricultural production. After July extensive play was given in the press and on the radio to the struggle centering on marketing and procurement of the harvest, but production per se seems to have been relatively free of direct disruption. [19]

Indirect influences continued, however, and the job of evaluating them is a difficult one. Whereas it is undeniable that port and rail tie-ups interfered with the supply of chemical fertilizers, insecticides, and other inputs to agriculture, it does not necessarily follow that "there is little doubt that the flow of tools, fertilizers, insecticides, and other production supplies was significantly below the 1966 level.[20] It must be remembered that a considerable amount of growth is built into these sectors of the Chinese economy by means of past investment and import decisions. Disruptions may have cut into the growth rate of agricultural supplies without actually causing their level to decline;[21] neither the pessimistic appraisal cited above nor the official claims of substantially

increased supplies are necessarily incompatible with the meagre facts
at our disposal.

A similar conclusion holds with respect to the decline in cadre
prestige and control in the villages. It is possible to argue on an a
priori basis that the net effect of this development was to delay farm
work, and lower the quality and quantity of work in the collective fields.[22]
On the same basis, it is possible to argue that if relaxation of Party control led to substantial recovery of agriculture after 1961, "one may well
assume that the same happened on a much bigger scale in many regions
at the end of 1966 and throughout 1967."[23] Some observers seem to regard the Chinese as caught on the horns of a dilemma with respect to
leadership of farm work; if leadership is strengthened, production must
suffer because peasant incentive declines, whereas if leadership is weakened, production declines because control falters. This sort of reasoning is formally (although not necessarily empirically) valid if one wants
to argue generally that the Communists can never elicit a superlative
performance from their peasantry, but it is clearly insufficient as a
basis for holding that production rose or declined at any particular time.

It is tempting to diagnose the state of supplies to agriculture by
reference to the estimated size of the harvest. But since assumptions
about supplies form one of the important ingredients of harvest estimates,
to do so would be to engage in circular reasoning. Independent information about inputs to agriculture, together with independent data on consumption levels, provide means by which the plausibility of output estimates can be checked. Dwight Perkins has evaluated various foodgrain
output estimates by such a method.[24] He concluded that "the grain estimates reconstructed from statements by Chinese officials plausibly reflect what we know of the performance of agriculture in China since the
disasters of 1959-61."[25] Since his paper appeared, the U.S. Agricultural Officer in Hong Kong has revised upward his estimates of foodgrain
production for the years 1964-1966, and a new set of alternative figures
has become available for 1967. It is worth repeating the exercise for
these new figures to see whether Perkins' conclusions are substantially
affected.

The results, together with sources and assumptions, are presented in Table 1, which compares the per capita foodgrain availabilities
implied by various combinations of assumptions about population growth,
old and new U.S. Consulate estimates, "official" estimates, and net
imports.[26] Three alternative assumptions about population growth after
1960 are used: a 1.5 percent growth rate, a 2 percent rate and the chang-

TABLE I

| | Population (Millions) | | | Foodgrain Output (mill. metric tons) | | | net food-grain import (mill. M.T.) | Per Capita Foodgrain Availability (Kg.) | | | | | | | | |
	1.5% growth rate	2% growth rate	Jones estimates	U.S. Cons. HK old	new	"Official"		U.S. Old at (pop. growth) 1.5%	2%	Jones	U.S. New at (pop. growth) 1.5%	2%	Jones	"official" 1.5%	2%	Jones
1960	676	676	676	160		150										
1961	686	690	680	167		162	3.0	243	242	246	(243)	(242)	(246)	232	230	234
1962	696	703	687	178		174	4.0	254	252	258	(254)	(252)	(258)	247	245	250
1963	707	717	697	179		183	4.3	259	256	263	(259)	(256)	(263)	259	256	263
1964	717	732	712	183	190	200	4.4	259	253	260	264	259	266	274	268	276
1965	728	746	728	180	185	200	5.2	257	251	257	265	259	265	282	275	282
1966	739	761	744	175	178	(205)	5.2	248	241	246	253	246	252	282	274	280
1967	750	777	760	175	187	230	4.1				249	241	246	296	286	292

Notes to Table I:

Population: the various population series begin from Edwin F. Jones' estimate for 1960; ignorance about population growth rates, as it is relevant to this exercise, concerns only the early 1960's. See Jones, "The Emerging Pattern of China's Economic Revolution," in An Economic Profile of Mainland China, studies prepared for the Joint Economic Committee of Congress, Vol. I, Table II, p. 93. It is rates which matter here, not absolute levels.

Foodgrain output: the original estimates of the U.S. Agricultural Officer in Hong Kong are contained in R. F. Emery, "Recent Economic Development in Communist China," Asian Survey, June, 1966, pp. 303-304, for the years 1960-1965. For 1966, estimates are given in John R. Wenmohs, "Agriculture in Mainland China-- 1967...", Current Scene, December 15, 1967, Table I, p. 10. Although Wenmohs refers to the 1966 figure as an upward revision, the original estimate is not given. For sources of "official" estimates, see Jones, op. cit., note to Table II, p. 93, and for 1967, Anna Louise Strong, Letters from China, No. 55, January 15, 1968. No "official" figure is available for the 1966 harvest, which was described only as being a record; I have arbitrarily guessed the figure used.

New Foodgrain Imports: Gross wheat imports are taken from James P. Rudbeck, "Communist Countries Take Less Wheat From Free World," Foreign Agriculture, U.S. Department of Agriculture, February 19, 1968. They are converted from bushels to metric tons at the standard rate of 27.215 kg. per bushel. They differ somewhat from earlier figures given by Robert L. Price and used in Perkins' article. Grain exports are taken from price for fiscal years 1961- 62 through 1965-66. They are assumed to have been the same in 1960-61 as in 1961-62, and the same in the two fiscal years 1966- 1968 as in 1965-66. They may actually have been slightly larger in both cases.

Net grain imports thus derived for fiscal years are divided in half and reconstituted to get rough approximations of calendar year imports. The assumption is made that all grain imports in fiscal 1960-61 occurred in calendar 1961. As a partial hedge against incomplete information for 1967, it is assumed that 500,000 tons more grain were imported in fiscal 1967-68 than we know about.

Per capita Foodgrain Availabilities: these figures consist of foodgrain outputs lagged one-half year, plus net imports, divided by population.

ing rates implicit in a population series suggested as plausible by Edwin F. Jones.[27] The last embodies an extremely low rate of less than 1 percent at the beginning of the decade, gradually rising to over 2 percent by 1965; it is extrapolated to 1967 at 2.2 percent.

The old U.S. Consulate estimates for both 1.5 and 2 percent rates of population growth are seen to imply small increases in per capita availability between 1960 and 1963 followed by gradual decline to 1966 levels comparable to those obtained in 1961. As Perkins points out, this result contradicts the available qualitative information indicating significant increases in consumption levels since the crisis year of 1961.[28] The Jones population series, which I have added, yields the same general result (See Table II). When the new Consulate figures are substituted for the old, per capita availabilities continue rising for another year or two before declining again. The biggest improvement between 1961 and 1966 is indicated by the series for 1.5 percent population growth, which shows the population increasing its available foodgrain per capita by 4 percent. But in 1967 all three series indicate little or no net gain above 1961 levels.

The "official" foodgrain statistics imply a steady rise in per capita availability, with a slight pause in 1966, at which point they stand from 19 to 22 percent higher than in 1961; by 1967 they are from 24 to 28 percent higher. Although impressive in comparision with the growth implied by the Consulate estimates, such increases are by no means exorbitant, and are in fact consistent with some independent evidence.[29] Use of the Jones population series does not affect this contrast; it merely results in somewhat faster initial recoveries in per capita availability due to very slow population growth in the early sixties. But it does not avoid the subsequent decline in the Consulate series to 1961 levels. The "official" output level for 1967 exceeds that for 1957 by only 24 percent, representing an average annual growth rate of 2.2 percent and little or no growth in per capita availability. In contrast, the Consulate estimate for 1967 implies that virtually no growth in output took place over the decade 1957–1967.

The conclusion then is that new Consulate estimates for the years 1964 to 1967 do not significantly alter the validity of Perkins' criticism. They continue to yield unreasonably low per capita availability levels relative to those prevailing in 1961, as well as implausibly low productivities for the substantially increased amounts of inputs to agriculture over the past decade. The performance suggested by "official" statistics, on the other hand, is not one of rapid growth, but of sufficient increase

TABLE II

	Percent Changes in Per Capita Foodgrain Availability		Percent Changes in Foodgrain Output	
	1961–66	1961–67	1957–67	1961–67
U.S. Consulate Old Estimates				
1.5% Pop. growth	+2			
2% Pop. growth	0			
Jones pops.	0			
U.S. Consulate New Estimates			+1	+12
1.5% Pop. growth	+4	+2		
2% Pop. growth	+2	0		
Jones pops.	+2	0		
"Official" Estimates			+24	+42
1.5% Pop. growth	+22	+28		
2% Pop. growth	+19	+24		
Jones pops.	+20	+25		

Source: Table I

to maintain low but adequate consumption standards, and a moderate but positive response of foodgrain output to increasing amounts of inputs. Moreover, China is recently reported to have bought less wheat from its Western suppliers in fiscal 1966-67 than in the previous fiscal year, and so far purchases for 1967-68 are lower still (although it is too early to ascertain their final amount).[30] Whereas 230 million tons may well turn out to overstate the harvest for 1967, it is difficult to imagine that China would be stabilizing her wheat imports, to say nothing of trending downward, if her production were as low as 187 million tons.

Foodgrain output is of course only one element in agricultural production. It has been emphasized--perhaps over-emphasized--here because of its symbolic importance as an indication of economic viability and because it is the subject of a wide divergence of views. Before concluding the discussion of agricultural conditions, however, something should be said about the state of economic crops as well.

Reports from Peking for 1967 leave the impression that they too had a good year: "most of the major industrial crops--such as cotton, oil-bearing seeds, sugar cane, sugar beets, bast fibre crops, and tobacco--and also fruit, silkworm cocoons, and livestock, exceeded all previous records in history and in some cases far surpassed them."[31] No figures were given for cotton, but it was announced that cotton purchased through September increased 8.7 percent over the same period in 1966,[32] and that Hopei province, which boasts the biggest cotton acreage in China, had increased its cotton crop by 30 percent.[33] Among the few other statistics released are included 10 percent increases in production of flue-cured tobacco, rapeseed, and hemp,[34] and an increase of 15 percent in the output of sugar cane and sugar beet.[35] China's sugar-growing center, Kwangtung Province, reported a considerable increase in cane output.[36] In line with this generally optimistic picture of economic crop production, Peking reports increased state purchases of such crops and record high purchases in Peking, Tientsin, Shanghai, Canton, Tsinan, and Harbin.[37] "Meats, vegetables, fruits, and other non-staple foods are available in greater quantities than before,"[38]

The claim of record numbers (or increase?) of livestock warrants attention, because of the poor supply of draft animals since the Great Leap. Draft animals are thought to have declined to about half their 1957 numbers by 1961 and to have recovered to only a little more than 60 percent by 1965. Although I have seen no figures regarding specific kinds of animals, the increase in the number of sheep is singled out as having been particularly impressive. Bigger increases than in 1966 are claimed for livestock in general in the major stock-breeding centers of Inner Mongolia, Sinkiang, and Tsinghai, as well as in Hopei, Honan, Kirin, Liaoning, and Heilungkiang. [39]

Of course the significance of agricultural output to planned development efforts depends not only on its size but also on the degree of control exercised by the center over it. Not only would we expect the aggregate investment rate to decline if such control slackens (since peasant consumption would probably rise), but the allocation of investment resources between different types of projects might also change. Some observers feel that Peking was seriously concerned with lagging grain procurement toward the end of 1967, when it acknowledged "agitation of peasants by class enemies to retain the farm crops instead of selling them to the state."[40] Much exhorting of the peasants to sell their surplus grain to the state took place from the end of the summer harvest on, but this subject has been perennially emphasized by the press at procurement time. How representative were the various reported incidents of peasants illegally dividing up, consuming, or burying their grain is impossible to say. China officially reported an increase in state purchases of grain (as well as other crops) over 1966.[41]

Industry

If agriculture seems by and large to have had a good year in 1967, there is less reason to be sanguine about the state of Chinese industry during the Cultural Revolution's more recent stages. Disruptions were frequent and occasionally prolonged, and they took their toll on the country's exports. Nevertheless, the problem of evaluating the general situation in industry is like that of agriculture. The Chinese reported a 20 percent increase in gross value of industrial production in 1966. Presumably in the absence of major disruptions there would have been a significant increase in 1967. Did the Cultural Revolution merely eat into the "normal" percentage increase in industrial production or was it sufficient to cause an actual decline compared with 1966? There seems to be no reliable way of answering this question as yet, and Peking has published no overall statistic for industrial growth in 1967.

Several technical and production breakthroughs occured in 1967, indicating continued progress in the favored growth sectors. The most spectacular of these was highlighted by China's first explosion of a hydrogen bomb on June 17, and by the testing of a guided missile for the first time. In another sphere, the production of an all-purpose, transistorized electronic computer was announced, as well as the construction of China's first ocean-going freighter in the 10,000 ton class, the Dongfeng.

Among products said to have increased their output over 1966 to varying extents are salt, clocks and watches, toothpaste, synthetic detergents, egg products, wines and spirits, clothing, headgear and footwear, hardware, leather goods, printing ink, and fountain and ball-point pens,[42] suggesting that light industry did better than heavy industry. I have seen no such list for heavy industrial products, although in September increases were claimed for the first half of 1967 in production of steel, electric power, petroleum, precision instruments, and machinery.[43] As stated earlier, farm machinery and tool production was said to have increased substantially in 1967. Mass demand for industrial consumer goods was up, and sales of sewing machines, radios, thermos bottles, enamel wash basins, and aluminum pots and pans rose by 15 percent.[44]

Progress reports were issued for various parts of the year for a number of provinces and municipalities. Chungkuo Hsinwen said that industrial growth had been especially notable in cities of medium size, and cited Tzu-kung Municipality in Szechwan and Tsingtao in Shantung as representative examples, with increases of 29 and 22 percent respectively.[45] Figures for the first eight months of 1967 were given for Shantung Province, indicating a 12.8 percent increase in gross value of industrial production over the comparable period in 1966 and the greatest absolute increase in six years, and for Kwangtung showing a 10 percent growth above 1966 and the greatest absolute increase since 1949. Tsinghai was said to have achieved a 7.37 percent increase for the first half over the first half of 1966. Shanghai reported a gross value of industrial production for the first half higher than that of 1966. Note the modesty of all the percentages given. Many places, like Shanghai, were not assigned percentages at all; in other cases, the increases were surprisingly small. The major Penchi coal mining complex, for example, achieved a record production 2.4 percent greater than 1966.[46]

The tentative and modest nature of these reports, combined with an absence of hard data for the major production centers in China for the entire year, suggest a degree of disruption in 1967 which Chinese industry had been able to escape in 1966. The significant incidents began at the end of that year and peaked with the "January Revolution" in Shanghai. Following New Year's day editorials in Jenmin Jihpao and Chiehfang Jihpao announcing extension of the Cultural Revolution into industry, factional clashes occurred in many industrial enterprises. Admonitions from the Central Committee to workers and cadres to maintain proper working hours, quality and concern for State property, and the growing peace-making role of the Peoples' Liberation Army throughout the spring, may temporarily have restored order in industry.

Nevertheless, beginning in May a second wave of disruptions occurred which featured walk-outs and clashes between rival worker factions at a large number of industrial enterprises. Places affected included Chengtu (early May to mid-June), Chengchow (May), Wuhan (mid-June through July), Nanchang and Foochow (June), Kirin (mid-July), Canton (mid-July to the year's end, with a period of calm during the November 15 - December 15 Autumn Commodities Export Fair), and others. Among major industrial plants and other installations reportedly affected were the Changchun Motor Vehicle Plant, Fushun coal mines, Taching oil field, Anshan iron and steel works, and Lanchow oil refineries. Of course there have also been widespread rail disruptions. [47]

Since last September, when Mao went on an inspection tour of North, Central-South and East China and issued his directives "fight self, repudiate revisionism," "there is no reason whatsoever for the working class to split..." and calling for the "correct treatment of cadres," a great deal of emphasis has been put upon forming alliances, combating anarchy, and promoting production. Nevertheless, subsequent press references to a strong rebirth of "counter-revolutionary economism"[48] and evidence of continued turmoil in various parts of the country suggested that the major tasks of consolidating and rebuilding for 1968[49] would require some time to accomplish.

Foreign Trade

In 1966, China regained her 1959 past peak foreign trade turnover of about $4.3 billion. A significant feature of this trade was the large advance it revealed in business with the West and Japan at the expense of the Soviet Union and Eastern Europe. China's exports to the first group increased by 20.5 percent to a level of $1,811 million, while her imports rose 14.4 percent to $1,494 million. [50]

It appears that final trade statistics for 1967 will show a substantially unchanged total volume of two-way trade concealing a marked reduction in Chinese exports which offset a further increase in imports and threatened to produce a small trade deficit for the first time since 1954. [51]

Trade with China's biggest partner, Japan, fell by about 10 percent from $621 million in 1966 to $557 million in 1967. [52] But the explanation seems to lie in changing market conditions (particularly the stiffening Western European competition) and political difficulties rather than in economic disruptions traceable to the Cultural Revolution. For example, Japan substantially increased the amount of fertilizer sold to China last year, providing 2.12 million tons of ammonium sulphate as against only 1.6 million in 1966. But she had to settle for a price reduction of over 30 percent because of Chinese success in buying 3 million tons of nitrogenous fertilizer from the European consortium NITREX three months earlier at very low prices. [53] Some Japanese were reported as interpreting the expulsion of three of their correspondents from Peking and the refusal to extend visas of Japanese trading representatives in China as responses to Prime Minister Sato's trip to Taiwan and South Vietnam, and to Tokyo's prohibition of the display of some scientific equipment at a scheduled exhibition in Tientsin on the grounds that the material was on the COCOM list. [54] More recently, Japanese refusal to make certain concessions in their China policy was referred to as a major obstruction in the progress of trade talks under way in Peking. [55] And a recent report by the government organization JETRO (Japan External Trade Recovery Organization) is said to have expressed alarm over the development of European competition for the Japanese market in China. [56] On the other hand, during the Autumn Trade Fair in Canton, Japanese traders contracted to sell China 350,000 tons of rolled steel, the largest volume in the history of post-war trade between the two countries. Furthermore, they expressed the expectation that rolled steel exports would soon reach one million tons. [57] Thus it seems safe to say that the role played by the Cultural Revolution in the decline of Sino-Japanese trade in 1967 must have been minor.

In contrast the fortunes of China's European trading partners waxed in 1967. Trade with West Germany, Britain, and Italy in particular increased over that of 1966, with much of the increase consisting of exports to China. [58] On the other hand, Chinese exports to (and through) Hong Kong fell markedly.

As reported above, China's purchases of wheat declined in fiscal 1966-67 to about 5,250,000 metric tons from the record level of 6,700,000 tons during 1965-66. Australia contracted to deliver 1 1/2 million tons during the second half of 1967. Canada agreed during the Autumn Trade Fair in Canton to sell China over 2 million tons to be delivered January through October 1968. France received a Common Market export subsidy which cleared the way for a sale of one-half million tons of wheat. [59] Including all of the Canadian sale, which extends beyond the limits of fiscal 1967-68, these sales together constitute a total of about 4.2 million tons of wheat for the new fiscal year.

In general, then, the trade picture for 1967 does not seem to have been as much affected by domestic turmoil as some earlier predictions indicated. Chinese exports absorbed the bulk of such influence as existed, undoubtedly reflecting to some degree the disruptions in indistrial production and factory management as well as recurrent transportation problems. Yet even here the degree of culpability of the Cultural Revolution is open to question. The possibility that the Chinese--having repaid debts incurred during the 1950's to the Soviet Union and various Eastern European countries and built up substantial foreign exchange balances--deliberately chose to reduce their trade surplus rather than tie up additional funds in reserves, cannot be automatically ruled out. [60] Meanwhile imports continued to grow, and China evinced continuing interest in purchasing the components of industrial construction--machinery and equipment, rolled steel, transportation equipment, and even British computers for use in economic planning--as well as large amounts of chemical fertilizer for agriculture.

General Observations

The argument is frequently made that the Cultural Revolution was not intended by its proponents to violate the constraints of economic viability. [61] Nor, on the other hand, does it appear that Mao had "boosting production" primarily in mind when the Cultural Revolution was launched, for its initiation came at a time when good agricultural progress and an upsurge in industrial production and capital construction were already under way. [62] In this respect, the Cultural Revolution differs markedly from the Great Leap Forward, which was launched partly as a response to fundamental bottlenecks to economic growth that had developed toward the end of the First Five Year Plan period. [63] Instead, the Cultural Revolution may be regarded as a response to the political and social implications of an economic policy, which had already achieved a good deal of success during the five or six years of its implementation. The policy itself had been pragmatically arrived at through a process of trial and error. It appears then, that the growth rate of the economy is not a short-run issue at stake in the debate, as it was at the time of the Leap.

Although the leaders of the Cultural Revolution have apparently striven to minimize its short-run disruptions to the economy, their objections to the social and political concomitants of the successful economic policy of the early 'sixties has left them vulnerable to charges of incompetence and guerrilla idealism with respect to their long-term economic ideas. Thus the economic viability of Maoism ultimately will depend on its political and sociological realism, for the analysis of which the economist's tool kit is not notably appropriate.

Simplified and briefly stated, the economic positions with which the "capitalist roaders" are taxed tend to favor decentralization of authority to the enterprise level in industry (this is oversimplified, as will be seen) and to the household level in agriculture, and acquiescence in the development of a market which would both govern the allocation of resources to a much greater degree than at present and reward participants materially to the degree that they respond to its dictates. Assuming that the objective of the Maoists is to achieve maximum economic growth (subject to the constraint that consumption , er capita not decline), then the effect of the decentralization measures cited above on three crucial variables must be analyzed: the resulting change in initial levels of total income; the change in the investment rate; and the change in the productivity of investment. Assuming further that the first and third variables are likely to be positive because of improved incentives, the second may well not be since the shift to a system emphasizing material incentives is likely to require a larger share of national production devoted to consumer goods. Thus, on these assumptions, it is impossible to predict by a priori theorizing the net effect of the "revisionist" or the Maoist program on the growth rate in a specific economic situation. It all depends.

Furthermore, even the assumptions about the first and third variables are not as self-evident as they may appear at first. Both market-oriented and planned systems are well known to lead frequently to mis-allocation of resources, particularly in conditions of economic underdevelopment. In either case, the question of the efficacy of introducing improved incentive systems cannot be separated from that of the rationality of the relative price structure. A single example may suffice to illustrate this point. In the immediate post-Great Leap Forward years, the major bottleneck to industrial production was the low level of agricultural output. Yet the effectiveness of material incentives led local handicraft and industrial workshops to produce construction materials and auxiliary products for which high and profitable prices were paid by urban factories, thereby diverting efforts from production of farm tools and implements which brought little profit but were sorely needed to increase agricultural output. The net effect of this allocation of activity on industrial production was probably negative. Better incentives to produce the wrong thing do not constitute an improvement.

Nor should common assumptions about incentives be accepted implicity. Barry Richman, who had an opportunity to study some 38 industrial enterprises in China in 1966, was inclined to see certain virtues in the egalitarian procedures he observed, especially for underdeveloped countries. [64] More recently, during the Cultural Revolution, several Japanese visitors to China have expressed similar views, in one case arguing that "rationalization was promoted and production was increased as a result of the Great Cultural Revolution. "[65] This is not to say that there is conclusive evidence that nonmaterial incentives are superior to material ones, only that the evidence is too varied to suggest automatic acceptance of the opposite conclusion. We are dealing here with patterns of human response sufficiently unfamiliar to the economist to warrant Professor Harvey Leibenstein's recent use of the term "X-efficiency" to characterize them. [66] Leibenstein cites some of the discoveries revealed in the literature on the importance of psychological factors in productivity:

> 1) up to a point, smaller working units are more
> productive than larger ones;
> 2) working units made up of friends are more pro-
> ductive than those made up of nonfriends;
> 3) units that are generally supervised are more ef-
> ficient than those that are closely supervised; and
> 4) units that are given more information about the
> importance of their work are more proficient than
> those given less information. A partial reason for
> these observed differences is probably the likelihood
> that individual motivation towards work is differently
> affected under the different circumstances mentioned. [67]

It is apparent that a broad spectrum of social phenomena affects the development of motivation and work efficiency, that the question of material incentives is but one relevant factor, and that it may even be in conflict with other such factors.

If for any of these reasons there is a serious possibility that a "revisionist" economic program would lead to a slower growth rate than a "Maoist" one, the implications for political stability must be explored. Would a vast peasantry, on which even the rapid development of the modern industrial sector in the fifties could not make significant inroads, remain quiescent in the face of slower growth, especially if accompanied by increasing class and status stratification? Since the peasant will in any case have to bear much of the burden of economic development, this is a crucial question.

Finally, we must challenge still another assumption--that the "Maoist" and "Liuist" programs can indeed be so simply characterized. With respect to some institutions (e. g. free markets and self-retained plots) the division between them is fairly clear, but this is not true for others. For example, Liu Shao-ch'i has been identified with promotion of a vaguely defined system of industrial "trusts" (t'o-la-szu), whereby "factories in the same industry would be interconnected and put under the leadership of the Party committee in the principal plant in the industry."[68] He was even accused of advocating:

> highly 'centralized' and highly 'monopolistic' 'trusts' 'all the way to the end'. For instance, he frenziedly raised the cry: 'The socialist economy should be more centralized and more monopolistic than the capitalist economy.'[69]

Such a proposal, if it was indeed made, has ambiguous implications for industrial efficiency. In particular, it is not clear whether it would increase enterprise freedom. Instead, the objective might be to enhance the power of the central Ministries at the expense of regional autonomy. The point is that we simply do not know enough at present to evaluate accurately such proposals or objections to them.

This is but a special example of the general problem of ignorance which impedes our understanding of the various economic aspects of the Cultural Revolution. For example, after the Great Leap, Mao has been described as advocating that flagging incentives to engage in collective production be revived by "giving fewer orders to the peasants and taking less grain from them," thus recognizing the peasant's natural desire to have a personal grain surplus for security.[70] In contrast to his policy of "storing grain among the people," the opposition, particularly T'ao Chu, has been accused of setting high purchase prices for foodgrains "in order to buy emergency grain reserves from the peasants."[71] Is the general objective of the Maoist position to reduce urban-rural interflow as an incentive for increased agricultural production, replacing it by allowing the peasant to retain a larger share of his output? Is such a policy a corollary of the emphasis on local development based on self-reliance? Is the policy of regional price equalization for inputs to agriculture (see the section on agriculture above) related to this, and does it signal a shift away from concentrating high-quality inputs in a relatively small "modernizing sector" and toward spreading them more evenly over the countryside? How significant in this debate are military considerations related to national security? All of these issues, crucial to an understanding of the economic significance of what is happening in China, must await far more information before thorough analyses can be attempted.

Whatever one's opinion of the economic issues that have been raised in China over the last two years, it seems evident from the foregoing discussion that the current revolution has not so far shaken the economy to the same extent as did its precursor of 1958-60. The Great Leap, by ignoring the links between inter-dependent sectors of the economy, wasting large quantities of resources in useless production, and deeply injuring the statistical system, caused structural damage with repercussions that substantially outlasted the Leap itself. The disruptions that have occurred up to now in the Cultural Revolution do not appear to have involved such damage. Therefore, provided relatively stable working conditions can once again be instituted and maintained, there seems to be no reason why the Chinese economy should not continue to grow.

Footnotes

1. Quotation marks are used throughout this paper around the word "official" when designating post-1957 harvest estimates because these estimates are revealed by the leadership through private conversations with foreign visitors, "leaks" via unofficial but authoritative sources, etc. Thus, they do not have full official status.

2. The estimate of the U.S. Agricultural Attache, John R. Wenmohs, is contained in his article "Agriculture in Mainland China--1967: Cultural Revolution vs. Favorable Weather," Current Scene, December 15, 1967.
   The figure of 230 million tons is conveyed in Ann Louise Strong, Letters from China, No. 55, January 15, 1968. Miss Strong is unlikely to have used an abolute figure unless it was based on official information. She qualifies the 230 million tons as "not counting all reserves kept by production teams." Although she refers to "tons", I have taken this to mean metric tons, the standard unit for measuring the grain crop.

3. Hsieh's speech is reported in Canton Wen-ko T'ung-hsun (Cultural Revolution Bulletin), published by the "820" News Agency of the Propaganda Department of Red Guard Headquarters of Public Organs of Canton Municipality, November 8, 1967, translated in SCMP No. 4076, December 8, 1967. Chou En-lai's speech is reported in Tzu-liao Chuan-chi (Special Reference Material Supplement), published jointly by the Propaganda Department of Kung-Ko-Lien of Canton and Red Flag of Kuang-chou Jih-pao, marked "internal material, not for external circulation," and translated in SCMP No. 4080, December 14, 1967.

4. See Editorial box preceding Wenmohs, op. cit.; See also Lois Dougan Tretiak, "Lively Rejoicing," Far Eastern Economic Review (FEER), January 4, 1968, for another citation of this reasoning.

5. SCMP, No. 4080, op. cit.

6. See, e.g., Choh-ming Li, The Statistical System of Communist China, Berkeley, 1962, p. 149.

7. Hsiangkang Chingchi Nienchien (Hong Kong Economic Yearbook), 1967, p. 37. We know the official estimate for 1966 to be something over 200 million metric tons. Assuming it to be 205 million M.T., the average annual rate of growth for the five years 1962-1966 would be about 4.8 percent. A further 4.8 percent increase in 1967 would have brought the

harvest to about 215 million M. T. A harvest of 230 million M. T. represents an increase of about 12 percent over an assumed 205 million M. T. for 1966. Those tempted to reject out-of-hand a percentage increase of this magnitude should bear in mind that India has claimed a 40 percent growth in foodgrain output in 1967, largely due to fine weather conditions, (See New York Times, "Economic Survey of Asia and the Pacific," January 19, 1968, p. 70,) and that weather is thought to have been excellent in China also. However, since Peking has claimed only a 10 percent increase for the summer crop, unless the autumn harvest increased substantially more than 12 percent it follows either that 205 million M. T. understates the 1966 output or that 230 million overstates that for 1967.

8. Wenmohs, Current Scene, op. cit.

9. China Reconstructs, October, 1967, p. 30.

10. NCNA, December 27, 1967.

11. NCNA, February 12, 1968.

12. NCNA, December 21, 1967. Also, Peking Review, No. 2, January 12, 1968.

13. China Reconstructs, October, 1967.

14. NCNA, December 27, 1967, which goes on to state: "There are now only a small number of areas which still cannot meet their own needs in foodgrains."

15. NCNA, December 2, 1967, reported in BBC Summary of World Broadcasts, December 13, 1967.

16. NCNA, December 27, 1968.

17. China News Analysis, No. 691, January 12, 1968, where Kiangsi radio in November and December is cited.

18. NCNA broadcast, November 29, 1967. BBC Summary of World Broadcasts, December 6, 1967.

19. John Wenmohs, "Agriculture in Mainland China--1967" op. cit., pp. 4, 5.

20. Wenmohs, op. cit., p. 4.

21. Some Taiwan specialists on Chinese agriculture are reported to believe that production in large and small local fertilizer plants was "at least sufficient to cover the temporary deficit created by the urban-based problems of the Cultural Revolution." See Lois Dougan Tretiak, "Lively Rejoicing," Far Eastern Economic Review, January 4, 1968.

22. Wenmohs, op. cit., pp. 1, 4.

23. CNA, No. 691, January 12, 1968. That free markets continue to exist and may even have been extended during this period is suggested by a broadcast of the Shantung Provincial Service in Mandarin, September 15, 1967, which stated that commune members "are allowed to sell and buy or exchange at the market the grain crops, fat - and oil - bearing crops which they privately own" at times other than periods of state purchase, when such private transactions are prohibited. The broadcast reiterates this stipulation, and also emphasizes that grain and oil-bearing crops raised collectively may only be sold to the state ("prohibition against the selling and buying of grain crops, cotton, cured tobacco, oil-bearing crops, hemp, and other items should be strictly enforced "), suggesting that such strictures are at times honored in the breach. What is interesting about this broadcast, however, is that some grain is allowed to be marketed privately; earlier laws prohibited private marketing for Group One commoditites altogether (a prohibition subject to periodic relaxation). See Audrey Donnithorne, China's Economic System, New York, 1967, ch. 11.

24. Dwight Perkins, "Economic Growth in China and the Cultural Revolution", The China Quarterly, No. 30, April-June, 1967.

25. Ibid., p. 39.

26. In a comment on Perkins' paper in The China Quarterly, No. 31, July-September, 1967, Werner Klatt criticizes Perkins for using gross per capita grain availabilities rather than a grain balance technique which would take into account shifts in the allocation of available grain among alternative uses. While there is no doubt that this method would yield a more accurate picture of actual consumption levels, Perkins convincingly argues that it would not change (and would in fact strengthen) the nature of the conclusions he draws. Briefly, the reason is that the evidence indicates an increase in the proportion of the grain crop absorbed by non-consumption uses since 1960-61, not a decrease. In addition,

estimates of the division of grain between various uses are even more tentative and uncertain than estimates of gross grain production. For these reasons, I have not attempted to construct a grain balance table for 1967.

It should be pointed out that some of my sources and assumptions differ somewhat from those used by Perkins.

27. See his "The Emerging Pattern of China's Economic Revolution," in An Economic Profile of Mainland China, Studies Prepared for the Joint Economic Committee of Congress, Vol. I, Table II, p. 93.

28. China Quarterly, No. 30, p. 38.

29. See Perkins, op. cit., p. 38.

30. Foreign Agriculture, U.S. Department of Agriculture, February 19, 1968.

31. NCNA, December 27, 1967.

32. Hsiangkang Chingchi Nienchien, p. 37.

33. NCNA, January 29, 1968.

34. Hsiangkang Chingchi Nienchien, p. 38

35. NCNA, October 27, 1967.

36. NCNA, December 2, 1967, BBC Summary of World Broadcasts, December 13, 1967.

37. NCNA, December 31, 1967.

38. "Home Market Brisk", Peking Review, No. 2, January 12, 1968.

39. "Excellent Situation in China's Livestock Production in 1967", NCNA, September 28, 1967, (SCMP, No. 4032).

40. Radio Peking broadcast reported by Charles Mohr, New York Times, December 22, 1967. See also Wenmohs, op. cit., pp. 8, 9.

41. NCNA, December 31, 1967.

42. Peking Review, January 3, 1968, "China Reaps All-Round Record Harvest." Note the absence of the major light industrial category of textiles from this list.

43. "A Discussion of China's Economic Situation," Chung-kuo Hsin-wen, Canton, September 23, 1967, tr. in JPRS, No. 43,252, November 7, 1967.

44. "Home Market Brisk", Peking Review, No. 2, January 12, 1968.

45. "A Discussion of China's Economic Situation," op. cit.

46. For the Penchi coal mines, see Jenmin Jihpao, December 28, 1967. For the other reports, see Hsiangkang Chingchi Nienching, pp. 38-40.

47. For a review of the industrial situation as described above, see "What Price Revolution: China's Economy in 1967," Current Scene, November 1, 1967.

48. See Chiehfang Jihpao, December 20, 1967, cited in Dick Wilson, "The China after Next," FEER, No. 5, 1968; for other such references, see China News Analysis, No. 695, February 9, 1968.

49. Jenmin Jihpao, January 1, 1968.

50. 20th Battle Act Report for 1967, Dept. of State, p. 59. Chinese exports are c.i.f., imports f.o.b.

51. See Sidney Klein, "The Cultural Revolution and China's Foreign Trade: A First Approximation," Current Scene, November 17, 1967, for a summary of statistics on Chinese trade up to that time and predictions for the whole year.

52. See dispatch by Tillman Durdin, New York Times, February 16, 1968.

53. Lois Dougan Tretiak, "On Bended Knee," FEER, September 28, 1967, p. 627.

54. FEER, September 28, 1967, p. 595.

55. New York Times, February 16, 1968.

56. FEER, No. 8, 1968.

57. Kyoto broadcast, December 15, 1967, BBC Summary of World Broadcasts, December 20, 1967.

58. New York Times, February 16, 1968, and Lois Dougan Tretiak, op. cit., p. 626.

59. See FEER, December 17-23, 1967, p. 528; New York Times, February 13, 1968; James P. Rudbeck, in Foreign Agriculture, February 19, 1968, p. 4.

60. I am indebted to Robert Dernberger for raising this point.

61. See, e.g., Perkins, China Quarterly, No. 30, pp. 43-46.

62. On this subject, see the testimony of Kang Chao before the Joint Economic Committee of Congress, "Mainland China in the World Economy," Hearings Before the Joint Economic Committee of Congress, Ninetieth Congress, First Session, U.S.G.P.O., Washington, 1967, pp. 134-142.

63. For a recent brief but interesting discussion of this point, see Shigeru Ishikawa, "Economic Problems of China," Chugoku Mondai no Bunseki (Analysis of Chinese Problems), Tokyo, 1966, tr. in JPRS 39,477.

64. "Capitalists and Managers in Communist China," Harvard Business Review, January-February, 1967.

65. See report of correspondent Samejima in Nihon Keizai, November 6, 1967; also Koichiro Matsuki, "Economic Aspects of China's Great Cultural Revolution," Economist, February 7, 1967, tr. in Summaries of Selected Japanese Magazines, February 20-27, 1967; Atsushi Motohashi, "Economic Aspects of the Cultural Revolution," Asahi Shimbun, May 18, 20-23, 1967; report of Japan External Trade Recovery Organization (JETRO), Delegation to China, Asahi Shimbun, June 20, 1967.

66. H. Leibenstein, "Allocative Efficiency Vs. 'X-Efficiency,'"American Economic Review, June, 1966, pp. 392-415.

67. Ibid, p. 402, Footnote references in this quotation have been deleted.

68. "Industrial Management in 1964-67," China News Analysis, No. 694, February 2, 1968, p. 2. This issue contains a summary of the controversy over "trusts."

69. Ching Kung, "The Plot of the Top Ambitionist to Operate 'Trusts' On a Large Scale Must Be Thoroughly Exposed," Kwangming Jihpao, May 9, 1967, tr. in SCMP, No. 3948, May 29, 1967, p. 3.

70. Anna Louise Strong, Letters From China, No. 55, January 15, 1968.

71. See Hsinhui Kungnungping Chanpao(Worker Peasant Soldier Combat Bulletin), No. 18, November 14, 1967; SCMP, No. 4083, December 19, 1967.

THE CULTURAL REVOLUTION AND CHINESE FOREIGN POLICY

Robert A. Scalapino

Introduction

The foreign policies of any major state are developed with three broad, interrelated objectives in mind: security, external influence and internal benefits. Ours is an age, moreover, when the range of alternatives--and problems--connected with each of these basic desiderata has expanded enormously.

These are times which encompass both "people's wars" and ICBM's, the innate primitivism of storming the barricades and the awesome sophistication of obliterating entire regions. These are also times when old fashioned colonialism seems completely archaic, existent only in a few enclaves, but where the interpenetration of one culture and state by another runs the widest possible gamut in terms of techniques and goals. Isolation has been rendered virtually impossible for all except the most insignificant and remote or the most authoritarian, those equipped to operate a garrison state with maximun efficiency. The more subtle forms of self-determination and independence (neutralism, for example) on the part of weak peoples and small political units everywhere are in jeopardy.

The dubious long-range viability of isolation, however, does not necessarily reduce its attractiveness in a period of unprecedented unheaval and danger. The issue of priorities, moreover, is a real and vital one for all governments. Most people at present are being subjected to a massive revolutionary experience, one affecting their personal lives in a profound sense. Since in its most immediate and obvious forms, this is an indigenous, even internal experience, issues of priority and interrelation between foreign and domestic policies are inevitable. At the level of the "average citizen" and the "other-involved" elite, this may take the form of xenophobia or pressures for simple withdrawal. At different levels, including that of the top political elite, it is likely to take more sophisticated forms: the reexamination and readjustment of external and internal commitments in accordance with discerned pressures and threats. Over time, this will probably lead to a wider, more complex range of foreign policy techniques, with each type or level of technique having been assessed as to cost and risk.

In any case, however, one central question of this era is likely to be how can foreign policy, in positive terms, underwrite domestic needs, symbolize the validity of one's internal policies, and abet the citizens' sense of pride and power? In negative terms, the same basic question can be put differently: how can foreign policy serve as a minimal source of added anxiety? Indeed, can it serve as a useful distraction from internal difficulties rather than becoming merely an additional source of grievance?

These are all relevant considerations for an analysis of Chinese Communist foreign policy, as for American or Soviet foreign policy. When the Chinese Communists came to full power in 1949, they brought with them a dual legacy--theirs and China's. These two legacies were more compatible than has often been realized, although they were certainly not identical. For example, the Chinese Communists possessed a curious combination of utopian internationalism and practical ethnocentrism. Their ideology was cosmic and universal, their experience relatively confined, China-centered, or more precisely, rural-centered, and replete with the values of puritanism, self-sufficiency, and antiforeignism. It is of enormous significance that Chinese Communism was in the hands of a very special type of rural gentry after 1930.

Traditional China also had its particular combinations of cosmic internationalism and narrow exclusiveness. As is well known, the very term for China, Chung-kuo or Central Kingdom, conveyed the sense of a larger universe revolving around a primary, directing force. In theory at least, anyone could change in status from barbarian to the ranks of the civilized by accepting Chinese values. However, the demand for a common standard--a Chinese standard--made insuperably difficult any adjustment to the norms of a Western-derived set of international relations that rested upon the concept of the sovereignty of separate, different, and equal states. The world of classical China was peopled by the superior and the inferior. It involved truth and error, power and weakness.

Indeed, in establishing the distinction between the barbarian and the civilized in the broader arena, and between the king and the tyrant at home, traditional Chinese leaders dealt with the problem of "error" in a fashion that casts a long shadow over Chinese Communist theory and practice. Barbarism is potentially and perhaps innately a political concept. As such, it need not encompass the totality of a foreign state. Differentiations within the state become possible. The method of making distinctions is clarified by means of a domestic example. One can never legitimately kill a king, for by definition a monarch holds the mandate of heaven. One can and should kill a tyrant, however, and a tyrant is a king unable to fulfill his role, having lost or never found the path of truth.

Such a legacy fits well with a considerable proportion of Chinese Communist foreign policy. Throughout the Communist era, there has been a strong temptation to deal not with states but with individuals or groups potentially capable of becoming civilized, that is to say, acknowledging Chinese (Maoist) values. Indeed, what is important is not relations among legal entities like states, but relations among legitimate forces. And who is legitimate? Here the distinction between "the people" and "the enemies of the people" becomes crucial. One cannot harm "the people," who by definition are those possessing the modern mandate of heaven, but one can and should silence "the enemies of the people," those who consciously resist the path of truth (in this case, Marx-Lenin-Maoism). Contradictions may exist among the people, but these can be resolved by patient dialogue. "The enemies of the people," however, must be destroyed in the same thorough fashion as one removed the tyrants of old.

It is not essential for our purposed to explore this matter in greater depth, or to examine other aspects of the dual legacy which Communist China inherited. It is sufficient to note that at least since the early nineteenth century, both the classical and the modern rulers of China have had to wrestle with the paradoxes implicit in attempting to carry relatively intense universalist and exclusivist values simultaneously. Indeed, classical China fell into ruin in no small measure because of the inability of the late Ch'ing era rulers to resolve or contain this problem.

There is no desire here to argue that current Chinese foreign policy can be correctly perceived merely by reference to tradition, or that Maoism has returned, full circle, to Confucianism. I do not belong to the "China is China is China" school. Obviously, the issue is more complex. In the first place, some proclivities can be shared by culturally different societies having certain comparable attributes. The problem of balancing universalist and exclusivist values takes on a special character in all continental-size societies, and one can find the dilemma clearly reflected in American and Russian, as in Chinese foreign policy. One should be exceedingly wary, moreover, of positing any theory of inevitability--or permanance--to the particular links which connect selected aspects of the past to the future. At certain points, modern Chinese leaders--communist and otherwise--<u>have</u> experimented with substantially different approaches or emphases.

For example, the early Republican period represented in the main an era of commitment to drastically different values from those generally associated with the traditional mix, both in foreign and domestic polices. In this period, a conscious effort was made to enter the universal stream, to accept the dominant international techniques and values. Sun Yat-sen, indeed, remains a symbol of that effort, despite subsequent attempts to use his image for diverse purposes. Moreover the Communists themselves, in the years immediately after 1949, made a serious effort once again to elevate an other-directed "universalism" to a position of dominance, albeit a Communist, not a Lincolnian "universalism." This was the time of the Soviet model, and a fulsome acknowledgment of the "socialist bloc led by the great Soviet Union."

That period passed, however, like the early Sun era before it, and once again, the unresolved issue of an internally directed universalism versus exclusiveness re-emerged in an insistent fashion. In this context, the classic issue--and classic responses--do have a meaning, because they represent that element within Chinese culture available to a troubled elite, capable of renewed influence both upon the style and the substance of foreign policy.

The Cultural Revolution and China's Security Policy

Let us begin by examining the impact of the Cultural Revolution upon the crucial question of Chinese security. In the formative period of Communist rule over China, down to 1957-1958, the new leaders of Peking appeared to be moving in the direction of an orthodox modernist-nationalist security policy, one with expansionist potential but easily comprehensible to external policy makers, communist and non-communist alike. A first crucial step was the alliance with the Soviet Union, consummated on February 14, 1950. By this action, China aligned itself with the second greatest power in the world, thereby obtaining major security at minimal cost, and being allocated also a sphere of influence in Asia, at least insofar as the Communist movement was concerned.[1] The next step was the modernizing of Chinese conventional military forces, a task both aided and retarded by the costly Korean War. Contrary to Peking's public claims, Chinese professional military men must have considered the price paid for a standoff in Korea as extraordinarily high. Losses may have reached one million Chinese dead, including a significant number of the seasoned veterans of anti-Japanese campaigns and the victorious civil war.[2] American fire-power had wrought enormous destruction upon the essentially primitive Chinese army. The Chinese, indeed, had lost the final, climactic battles of April and May 1951 with frightful casualties.

Thus, the Korean War presented a compelling argument for policies of military modernization and extreme caution in confronting the United States in direct combat. In any rapid modernization program the Soviet Union would have to play a significant role, not merely with respect to equipment but in a wide range of training and supplementary activities as well. Modern Russian weapons, Soviet advisers, and intensive training courses were now crucial elements in Chinese military development. Professionalization took many forms from the establishment of ensignia and rank designations to the training of specialists in such fields as rocketry and chemical warfare. One must also assume that contemporary Soviet theories of military tactics and strategy, most of them at strong variance with Maoist theory, penetrated deeply into Chinese military thinking.[3]

In essence, Russian military concepts were based upon the premise that the conflict against which precautions had to be taken was one pitting large-scale military forces against each other, and involving almost the totality of the civilian populations as well. Such massive conflict could not be sustained over any considerable period of time. Indeed, the decisive actions might take place in the initial period. The premium was thus upon maximum preparedness and modernization at all levels. In contrast, Maoism, reaching into its own traditions and those of classical China, is based upon the premise of protracted warfare, a mobilized citizenry, and the primacy of politics over weaponry. Maoism represents the gamble that backwardness can be converted into an asset even in the late twentieth century if one is prepared to take full advantage of the opponent's psychological and political weaknesses, and use with equal skill one's own topographical, cultural, and political strengths.

The open conflict between these two theories of security was first joined in the 1957-58 period as part of a rising "Maoist" assault upon the Sovietization of Chinese Communism, an assault which encompassed the economic and political arenas as well as the military one. The counterattack took the form of The Great Leap Forward, Mao's most ambitious venture into mobilization politics. In its impact upon Chinese military leaders dedicated to professionalism, the Great Leap posed a series of

frontal challenges. To involve the army deeply in both economic production and political activities was to blur its functional role, reduce its
military efficiency, and retard the general modernization process. To
send officers into the ranks for a one-month stint as common soldiers
and other "equalizing" measures were actions threatening not only spe-
cialization but discipline as well.

As might have been expected, certain key figures within the Chinese military establishment resisted, with the knowledge, sympathy,
and support of the Soviet Union. The first act of the drama ended in the
fall of 1959, with the Maoists winning a significant victory. The Lushan
meeting of the Party Central Committee, held in August, seemingly involved an open and broadly ranging attack upon party policy by Marshal
P'eng Teh-huai, Minister of Defense.[4] P'eng and his supporters trench-
antly criticized the Party for major economic failures. Almost certainly,
however, military issues--including questions of nuclear policy--were
close to the center of the controversy in addition to political and economic
policies.

At this point and henceforth, the nuclear issue would cut several
ways. Rapid Soviet progress in the nuclear field certainly stimulated
Chinese expectations of Russian performance in the international field.[5]
After the successful testing by the Soviet Union of an ICBM and the orbit-
ing of an earth satellite in the fall of 1957, Peking's leaders took the
position that the USSR now could and should challenge the United States
more forcefully when the interests of the Communist world were at stake.
Disillusionment with subsequent Khrushchevian foreign policies was thus
all the more intense.

At the same time, the major strides made by the Russians in the
whole field of nuclear weaponry must have made the prospect of any break
with Russia extremely painful, especially to those Chinese military leaders
who viewed modernization as crucial and who had worked closely with
Soviet counterparts for some years. Would extensive Soviet support not
be vital for at least a decade? Under these condtions, decisions respect-
ing relations with the Soviet Union after 1957 must have been terribly
difficult, with numerous nuances of difference developing.

It would seem safe to assume that despite the growing differences
with respect to Chinese security policies during this period, there was
general agreement upon the desirability of China's acquiring an independent nuclear capacity. There may have been some Chinese leaders who
preferred to concentrate exclusively upon conventional modernization

and continued reliance upon the Soviet nuclear umbrella, but it is likely that the prevailing professional view was that the development of a wide range of nuclear weapons, including tactical weapons, was an inevitable and desirable development within the general modernization program, to be protected by an ultimate reliance upon Soviet power in the event of confrontation with the United States. One's attitude toward Sino-Soviet relations, however, would relate to the costs and the timing of Chinese nuclear development. Without Soviet assistance, the development of Chinese nuclear capacity was certain to interfere more extensively with the process of conventional modernization.

But whereas many professional military men probably saw the development of nuclear capacity as a logical aspect of a general modernization program, there are indications that "good Maoists" saw nuclear weapons in some measure as a substitute for broadly gauged military modernization, a modern increment that could be meshed with "people's war" theories. Nuclear weapons would at once provide China with major power status and raise the threshold of risk to the United States, thereby enabling "people's wars" to unfold in Asia with ever greater protection against external interference and ever greater hope of external support. Thus, we may presume that all parties to the controversy greeted the Sino-Soviet accord of October 15, 1957, with great satisfaction. In that accord the Soviets apparently agreed to provide China with the necessary techniques for nuclear weapons, including a sample atomic bomb. [6]

Two years later, however, it was clear that a majority of the Chinese Communist leaders were prepared to go it alone, rather than to compromise with internal and external opponents. The year 1958, of course, had been a crucial one, with a series of international crises, including a second major crisis over the offshore islands, with the Soviet Union indicating a clear reluctance to become involved in a Far Eastern war with the United States on behalf of China. Khrushchev's stock dropped precipitously in Peking during this period. In September 1959, P'eng and Huang K'o-ch'eng, Chief of Staff of the Army, were removed and replaced by Lin Piao and Lo Jui-ch'ing respectively. For the next five years, on the surface at least, the Maoists appeared to be in strong control of the military establishment. While there were retreats from some of the excesses of the 1957-1959 era, in general, the politicization of the Chinese military was heightened in a great variety of ways. The thought of Mao became an all-pervasive force as it was projected to military men--from the raw recruit to the aging general. That thought emphasized men over weapons, red over expert, and the doctrines of people's wars. Meanwhile, nuclear efforts were pushed forward with all possible speed, and in October 1964 the Chinese detonated their first nuclear device.

The 1965 crisis within top Chinese military-political circles, however, revealed clearly that the issues involved in P'eng's dismissal continued to divide key figures within the Communist hierarchy. The crisis was triggered by a fear that the escalating Vietnam war would soon engulf China. The issue appears to have been posed largely in defensive terms: what if the United States, having commenced the bombing of North Vietnam, elected to strike against China, a major source of supplies for the North Vietnamese? As a result of recent Maoist polemics against Liu Shao-ch'i, P'eng Teh-huai, and Lo Jui-ch'ing, we know now the crucial lines of the debate, at least from the Maoist standpoint.

Confronted with the danger of an imminent American attack as they viewed it, men like Lo Jui-ch'ing were prepared to "capitulate" to the Soviet Union, re-entering a united front "on revisionist terms," thereby sacrificing true Marxism-Leninism. To render this palatable, "the revisionists" constantly dwelt upon the horrors of war and the extreme danger in which China found herself. Further, like their Soviet brothers, they were prepared to subordinate politics to military science, turning a proletarian army into a bourgeois army. Like all "opportunists," Lo and others regarded weapons as the ultimate power. They were "against arming the masses, against the militia training system, and against the Chairman's great strategic thinking on people's war."[7]

It would be fascinating to know whether the United States unwittingly played the crucial role in the downfall of Lo Jui-ch'ing and others of his persuasion. By the end of 1965, American officials had used a variety of means to attempt to convince Chinese leaders that the United States did not intend to attack China and did not wish war with China-- but that if such a war came through Chinese initiative, there would be no privileged sanctuaries. Perhaps the Maoists needed scarcely more than this assurance to launch a giant "purification" campaign both within and outside military circles. In any case, by 1966, major opponents including Lo Jui-ch'ing had been purged, and Maoist military tenets had been made once again a supreme test of loyalty and one's capacity to be called a true Marxist-Leninist.

Today, Communist China's professional military leaders stand in the shadow of the old guerrilla fighter, Mao Tse-tung, who is gambling that his knowledge of revolution, human psychology, and the diverse cultural values of his primary opponents is sufficient to defeat any forces raised against him, and to win the ultimate victory via a world revolution. Four major premises underlie Maoist military tactics and strategy. First, his strategy is intimately linked to a rising crescendo of revolutionary success throughout the world. Mao does not conceive of Chinese security apart from the prevalence of the East wind over the West, and this explains the combination of defensive and offensive elements that pervade his military tactics. Like the Lenin whom he so much admires and who fashioned Bolshevik tactics in the Soviet Union's era of internal weakness, Mao sees a global revolution, not nation-to-nation competition, as China's route to power.[8] This gives to his doctrine a unique militancy: "The seizure of power by armed force, the settlement of the issue by war, is the central task and the highest from of revolution. This Marxist-Leninist principle of revolution holds good universally, for China and for all other countries."[9]

Nor does the universalism implicit in Maoist doctrines stop here. China under Mao has perfected the precise revolutionary model that can be used throughout the late twentieth century world. Be it the jungles of the Congo, the arid plains surrounding Israel, or the densely packed Negro ghettos of America, they are those who, armed with the thought of Mao Tse-tung and adapting it creatively to their own conditions, are pursuing "people's war," mobilizing the whole of "the people," and emasculating their enemies--first politically, then psychologically, and finally militarily.[10]

The basic features of Maoist military tactics and strategy all derive from a sense of weakness, a feeling engendered in Mao throughout a lifetime of revolutionary experience. Hence the theme of man over weapons, and the ultimate primacy given the political element; hence the emphasis upon staying capacity--the protracted war. The frontal clash with current Soviet military theory was inevitable because Maoism stops short of the post-revolutionary era. It has not conceptualized power and success. In this most basic sense, Mao remains a permanent revolutionist. A master of mobilization politics in military as in civil affairs, he has built not a single institution whose survival capacities look good.

The absence of any concept of leading from strength within Maoist military doctrine contributes mightily to a third premise, namely, that China can apply steadily increased political-military leverage in the contemporary world and still maintain a minimal risk position vis-a-vis its central opponents, the Soviet Union and the United States. Consequently, it is not correct to categorize current Chinese military tactics as either "defensive" or "offensive." Obviously, the Maoists think in defensive terms in contemplating a struggle with either of the two super powers and never was that defensive imagery more colorfully drawn than by Foreign Minister Ch'en Yi when he reportedly remarked, "If the U.S. imperialists are determined to launch a war of aggression against us, they are welcome to come sooner, to come as early as tomorrow. Let the Indian reactionaries, the British imperialists, and the Japanese militarists come along with them. Let the modern revisionists act in coordination with them from the North! We will still win in the end. .. For 16 years we have been waiting for the U.S. imperialists to come in and attack us. My hair has turned grey in waiting. Perhaps I will not have the luck to see the U.S. imperialist invasion of China, but my children may see it, and they will resolutely carry on the fight."11

This defensive quality, however, should not obscure the offensive elements implicit in Maoist doctrine and tactics. No theory that proclaims the settlement of issues by war as the central task of these times and that berates the Soviet Union for its paltry aid to the revolutionary peoples of the world can be considered devoid of commitments of an offensive character--moral, political, and material. That these commitments, other than in verbal form, are presently being executed in a cautious manner merely represents a correct assessment in Maoist terms of communist versus enemy capacities. Indeed, it is precisely the combination of defensive-offensive elements in Maoist military doctrine that represents the tactical flexibility long a hallmark of the Maoist method. "The enemy attacks, I retreat. The enemy retreats, I attack." In this, as in other respects, the strategy of protracted war pioneered in China is projected for the world.

Maoist nuclear programming must be read in the same light. At this stage at least, its purpose is overwhelmingly political: first, to attain major power status, particularly in the eyes of the Afro-Asian world; second, to undermine the general position of the United States in Asia by casting doubt upon our credibility as an ally and raising the potential risks of alliance with America.

As one surveys Maoist security doctrines, once again the elements of universalism and exclusiveness lie uneasily together, testimony to the rival forces with which Chinese leadership--communist or otherwise--has always contended. The isolated, defensive, internal imagery evoked in such a picturesque manner by Ch'en Yi suggests a central kingdom beset by barbarians. But the expansive, cosmic tone of Maoist revolutionary theory suggests a concept of security interrelated to a universal movement with China serving as its source-spring.

Ironically, however, Maoism may soon be in the hands of professional military men. Even now, it is the hard-bitten army veterans like Huang Yung-sheng who are charged with administration and the keeping of the peace at the all-important provincial level.[12] Will those who follow Mao interpret China's security needs in the same manner, and via the same techniques as the old guerrilla-revolutionaries?

The Cultural Revolution and China's External Influence

Let us turn now to the critical issue of external influence, a second major element in Communist China's foreign policy objectives. At the outset, it is interesting to note the juxtaposition of China and India vis-a-vis the external world in 1950, and then note the contrasting picture a decade later. When the Chinese Communists came to power, they had emerged from a long period of relative isolation, and initially, their primary relations were with the Soviet Union. The Afro-Asian world was largely unknown territory. India, on the other hand, under Nehru, had moral and political influence throughout the Asian and African area, and very minimal relations with the Soviet Union. A decade later, the situation was almost completely reversed. Peking's leaders had succeeded in extending the influence of China very widely in Asia and Africa, while their relations with the Soviet Union had become both limited and hostile. India, with Nehruian foreign policy in ruins, now depended extensively for its security upon the Soviet Union (and the United States), but its influence upon the Afro-Asian region had sharply deteriorated.

Perhaps no aspect of Chinese foreign policy is as enigmatic, therefore, as the seeming unconcern with international opinion, particularly in official Asian and African circles, that has marked it at certain stages of the Cultural Revolution. Chinese involvement with the emerging world prior to the Cultural Revolution was substantial at many levels, especially when one considers the extraordinary needs at home for human and material resources. Up to 1966, Communist China had dispensed approximately one billion dollars (in U.S. dollar equivalent) in foreign assistance and aid.[13] The precise number of foreign students who have studied in China is unclear, but it would seem possible that as many as 10,000 have been short- or long-term residents. At the time when all foreign students were ordered out of the country, on September 20, 1966, there were approximately 1,000 foreign students in the country, excluding some 2,000 overseas Chinese.[14] By the end of 1965, moreover, Peking had diplomatic representation in forty-eight countries.

This situation had been drastically altered by the end of 1967. Chinese foreign aid had fallen to almost zero, although work continued on some aid projects previously commenced, and a few new offers had been initiated. There were practically no foreign students in the country. Almost all key diplomatic officials had been recalled "for consultation" in 1966, and even at the end of 1967, many embassies were being operated by chargé d'affaires. More dramatic, of course, had been the rising cycle of attacks--first upon Western culture, then upon foreign embassies and individual foreigners, culminating in the unprecedented events of July and August 1967 when both within China and abroad, a series of incidents were fomented. Among these were the attack upon a Soviet ship in Dairen harbor, the burning of the British legation chancery building in Peking, and incidents abroad involving a wide range of nations from Kenya to Switzerland. Indeed, in the twelve months prior to September 1967, Communist China had been involved in some type of crisis or incident with thirty-two nations, excluding the United States-- where ironically, contacts at Warsaw had remained correct, if not cordial.

The most obvious result of Chinese Communist actions was a precipitous drop in Peking's prestige,and the creation of a decidedly unfavorable image in many quarters of the world, including areas which Peking had previously sought to cultivate. One need recount only a few incidents to reveal the general picture. In Ceylon, the Prime Minister, Mr. Dudley Senanayake, in a statement before parliament on August 22 with reference to Chinese charges that Ceylon was engaging in activities which "the Chinese people absolutely cannot tolerate," announced that Ceylon "would not be bullied or badgered."[15] In Kenya, after the Kenyan Embassy in Peking had been besieged by Red Guards, some government officials recommended a closing of the Embassy and efforts to obtain exit visas were begun.[16] The Afghanistan government had to insist that anti-Soviet and anti-U.S. propaganda be removed from the Chinese embassy showcase in Kabul. The Swedish government protested the manhandling of its cultural attaché in Peking, but the protest was rejected as "distorted." In Japan, Communist China now appeared regularly as the nation most disliked in a leading public opinion poll.[17]

Some less obvious results of Cultural Revolution diplomacy were perhaps equally serious. Communist China not only appeared to be abandoning the accepted norms of international diplomacy, including protection for diplomatic officials and communications written in diplomatic language,[18] but it also operated in such a fashion as to make a clear reading of its signals impossible. Although this was not an entirely new development, by 1966-1967 Chinese official language had reached such a level of violence or threat as to render completely uncertain the relation between speech and action.

For example, in attacking the Swiss policy of allowing Tibetan refugees to operate in that country, a vituperative note from Peking ended with the statement: "This reveals more clearly the reactionary features of the Swiss government which, in collusion with imperialism, revisionism and reactionism, makes itself an enemy of the Chinese people. The Chinese people who are armed with Mao Tse-tung's thought, are not to be trifled with."[19]

Or one may observe the wording of the note of August 22, 1967, to the Ceylonese government which included the sentence: "The Ceylon Government headed by the United National Party has always played with counter-revolutionary dual tactics, saying one thing but doing another. If you refuse to come to your senses and continue to frenziedly oppose China, you must be held responsible for all the grave consequences arising therefrom."[20]

And toward the Tunisian government, "Standing on the side of U.S. imperialism, the Tunisian Government has been endeavoring to split and disintegrate the Arab peoples' anti-imperialist front. This has boundlessly enraged the Tunisian and other Arab peoples and encountered their resolute opposition. The Tunisian Government will certainly come to no good end."[21]

One could recite countless other examples, many of them repeating the same basic phrases: you will come to no good end; you will be held responsible for the grave consequences; your own people and the people of China will not stand for this. Not surprisingly, it was the recipient governments generally who refused to stand for such treatment. Chinese notes were curtly rejected. Embassies and legations in Peking were closed. And in a few extreme cases, diplomatic relations were completely broken. Even with Cambodia, events had come to a critical turn by September 1967.

How was it possible that men as urbane as Ch'en Yi and Chou En-lai had permitted such a debacle? The basic answer, of course, is that in the most critical periods, these men were not in charge of Chinese foreign policy. If we may rely upon the general accuracy of a wide range of wall posters and Red Guard newspapers, we can reconstruct many aspects of the struggle to control the Ministry of Foreign Affairs, a struggle which reached its climax in mid-1967, was exceedingly bitter, and laid bare a number of major issues in foreign policy, both of style and of substance.

The first attacks upon Foreign Minister Ch'en Yi appeared in Peking wall posters in October 1966. He was accused of suppressing the Cultural Revolution in the Ministry of Foreign Affairs, and his wife and son were also charged with various crimes. Ch'en produced a self-confession on January 24, 1967, before more than 10,000 Foreign Ministry personnel. Thereafter, he garnered support from Chou En-lai and Chiang Ching, and the attacks abated.[22] However, the assault was resumed in April 1967, with massed Red Guards demonstrating outside the Ministry on April 8.[23] The anti-Ch'en campaign mounted in intensity, and on two occasions in May, the offices of the Ministry of Foreign Affairs were temporarily occupied by Red Guard groups. Despite June wall poster statements that Ch'en had been cleared by Chou En-lai and Chen Po-ta, demands for Ch'en's ouster continued to pour forth from Red Guard critics. Even the Cultural Revolution Advisory Group may have been divided, and in August, under conditions approaching chaos, struggle meetings against Ch'en Yi were authorized. Two were held, on August 11 and August 27, involving thousands of witnesses. Ch'en was reportedly treated roughly on both occasions, and at one point, had to be protected by PLA soldiers.

During August and September, Ch'en Yi ceased to act as Foreign Minister, and during a portion of this time he may have been in the hospital as a result of his prolonged ordeal. One Red Guard newspaper of November 1967 quoted Mao as having said, "How can Ch'en be struck down? He has been with us 40 years and has so many achievements. He has lost 27 pounds in weight. I cannot show him to foreign guests in that condition."[24]

Whether this is an accurate quotation, of course, cannot be determined, but it does appear that the final decision of the top group around Mao in a period of intense political maneuvering was that Ch'en Yi could be criticized, but not overthrown. Presumably, his strongest supporter was Chou En-lai, and it was Chou who finally took direct charge of the Foreign Ministry, reportedly in late August. Prior to that time, there is some evidence that power had actually been seized by an extremist Red Guard element, with the immediate leadership being provided by

Yao Teng-shan, a younger diplomat who had earlier been ousted from
Indonesia. Behind Yao may have stood Wang Li of the Supreme Cultural Revolution Advisory Group, later to be ousted on charges of left
extremism.

It appears that the extremists first seized control temporarily
in January 1967, and many veterans--such as the Deputy Director of
the Political Department of the Ministry, Wang Ping--came under fierce
attack. [25] Evidently the "conservatives" fought back, and with some
success. "Revolutionary rebels" were reportedly pushed out of some
departments, and such individuals as Hsiao Chien, Section Head of the
American and Australian Department were reportedly holding firm
against the intrusion.

If these accounts from Red Guard sources are reasonably correct,
as seems likely, the Foreign Ministry must have been in turmoil inter-
mittently from at least January to September 1967, with some truly
extraordinary events taking place. For example, on May 29 some 300
Red Guards, one of two rival units from the Commission for Overseas
Chinese, broke into the Ministry, scaling the walls of the inner court
after having beaten up the guards at the entrance. Reportedly, they
forcefully opened two safes in the building and took out classified materials, then demanded that Liao Cheng-chih, the Director of the Commission for Overseas Chinese, be handed over to them for criticism.

Chou En-lai himself, on September 2, 1967, supposedly asserted
that power had been wrongly seized at the Foreign Ministry in August
by a Red Guard faction from the Peking Foreign Languages Institute, and
that this group withdrew only when ordered to do so by the Party Central
Committee. In the meantime, Red Guard elements had sent telegrams
directly to foreign embassies and carried on other types of activities,
with Yao Teng-shan taking the lead. Chou reportedly asserted that he
had criticized Yao directly, partly because in the place of a slogan authorized by the Central Committee, "Down with Liu, Teng,and T'ao," Yao
had put forth the slogan, "Down with Liu, Teng and Ch'en." Yao, asserted Chou, had thereby put himself above the Central Committee. [26]

It must be emphasized that these details all come from Red Guard
newspapers and wall posters. They may be inaccurate or exaggerated
in some degree, and it is very doubtful that they present the whole truth.
Nevertheless, they are sufficiently in accord with other sources to warrant general acceptance. And, if essentially correct, they shed a great
deal of light upon the bizarre character of Chinese diplomacy throughout

most of 1967. Put simply, Red Guard extremists displaced professional diplomats, or cowed them, for a portion of this period, especially at such critical times as the attacks upon the Soviet ship in Dairen and the burning of the British legation.

More light on the issues can be obtained by examining the reports of the charges against Ch'en Yi and his various self-criticisms and disclaimers.[27] The broad charge against Ch'en, of course, was that he had followed "the counter-revolutionary bourgeois line of Liu and Teng." He was also charged with having bureaucratic leadership proclivities, an erroneous ideology, and of having praised the intellectuals in exaggerated fashion and evaluated their talents too highly.

In specific terms relating to foreign policy, Ch'en was accused of having promoted the reactionary diplomatic line of the "three capitulations and the one extinction", policies supposedly fostered by Liu and Teng. This line is one of "capitulation to imperialism, revisionism, and the reactionaries of all countries and the extinction of the fire of the people's revolution in all countries."[28] Ch'en's attackers dug back into the records of the 1950's and 1960's to find instances when he had underestimated the American threat or even hinted at the possibility of some improvement in Sino-American relations. Using scraps of speeches, they then charged that the Liu-Teng-Ch'en line was in essence a pacifist line which aimed at extinguishing all national liberation movements.

Moreover, Ch'en had objected to the tactic of propagating Maoism abroad. Allegedly, he had asserted that the thoughts of Mao Tse-tung were innately Chinese, and for internal use. They would not be accepted abroad, he insisted, and the attempt to distribute Maoist literature and badges in foreign countries could only produce resentment.[29] It was also claimed that he had supported a "capitulationist" policy with respect to the overseas Chinese in Indonesia, Burma, and other areas, even suggesting that when Southeast Asians had chased off the Western imperialists we cheered, but when they seek to chase us off we make a fuss.

The character of these criticisms reveals clearly some of the basic foreign policy issues that emerged in the context of the Cultural Revolution. It should be emphasized at the outset that there is no way to tell how much support the "extremist" positions had from top Maoists, including Mao himself. We can, however, assert that the general course of the Cultural Revolution lent itself to powerful elements of exclusiveness and universalism, some new, many old, all intense. In its strong xenophobia, nationalism, and ethnocentrism, the Cultural Revolution manifested exclusiveness in forms scarcely equalled in the modern world. The initial attack upon Western culture within China was followed by assaults--verbal and physical--upon foreign representatives or states representing a striking parallel with the Boxer era. The militant stance with respect to the overseas Chinese, including the insistence that even if they are citizens of another state they must be allowed to express their loyalty to Chairman Mao was but one indication among many of a strident nationalism that spilled over China's boundaries. And the attempt to portray "the masses of the world" as avidly reading Mao's collected works and standing in adoration of this great man was one manifestation of an ethnocentrism so extreme as to be ludicrous at times.

Yet this same myth of the global masses worshiping Mao was a part of the universalist quotient that also projected itself formidably into the Cultural Revolution. The export of Maoism was the most overt expression of China's claim to be the sole legitimate source of the international revolutionary movement of our times. Repeatedly, Chinese spokesmen insisted that Mao was the current successor to Marx, Lenin, and Stalin, and thus the only true spokesman for the revolutionary people of the world.[30]

In theory at least, it mattered not that governments fell away from China. The primary issue was not among states, but between people and their enemies. As long as China under Chairman Mao retained the people of the world, Chinese diplomacy was successful. If the Soviet Union was currently governed by a Khrushchevian clique, the people of Russia would ultimately seize the red banner of Maoism and overthrow the revisionists. If the United States was under imperialist reactionaries, the progressive people of America would create their own people's war, with the suppressed blacks in the vanguard. It did not matter that the Ne Win and Suharto governments were Fascist, because the Burmese and Indonesian peoples, armed with the thought of Mao, would ultimately prevail.

Thus, at its height, the Cultural Revolution had so fused foreign policy and revolution as to make them practically indistinguishable. From that height there has now been some retreat. At least some of the extremists of the past have been removed from power. Under Chou En-lai's aegis, Ch'en Yi appears to be functioning once again. The attacks upon embassies and foreigners have ceased, and directives have been issued strictly prohibiting unauthorized actions of this sort. But at this point, it is by no means clear how far the retreat will go, or how effectively it will be enforced. Exclusiveness in a variety of forms is still pronounced. And the call for people's wars, the sharp attacks upon most of the governments of Asia, and the continued insistence that Maoism is the global wave of the future testify to the attraction which universalism continues to hold.

In objective terms, the People's Republic of China has paid heavily for its erratic behavior of the recent past. Its prestige in the non-Western world is the lowest within a decade, and this has affected such issues as the United Nations membership question. The international organizations which it once valued are now either hopelessly split, or abandoned. Its capacity to render aid, or even to make credible threats, has been greatly reduced. Yet is it possible that these blows are of less significance than one might suppose to men like Mao, who place first priority on winning the battle for China, under the assumption that if the revolution is made secure there and efforts to restore capitalism fail, the Chinese model will shine forth like a beacon light to the world, and all temporary setbacks in foreign policy can easily be recouped.

Internal Effects of Chinese Foreign Policy
During the Cultural Revolution

With this in mind, let us look briefly at Chinese foreign policy as it relates to internal benefits. Put succinctly, does Chinese foreign policy in its present form bolster the Maoist domestic program or threaten it? To draw up a balance sheet on this subject is more complex than might appear to be the case. The debit side of the ledger seems relatively clear. However tight the control over external news, the fact of China's declining prestige could scarcely have been kept from discerning citizens, especially groups like the intelligentsia. When Albania alone can be set forth as China's great ally, and attacks are even levelled against North Korea and the Japanese Communist Party, doubts as to Mao's universal appeal must be widespread.

At this point, moreover, morale within the professional foreign service must be at a very low ebb. The struggles of the last two and a half years, and particularly those within the Foreign Ministry over the past fourteen months, must have created havoc with the efficiency, self-confidence, and esprit-de-corps of the organization. Within each group and subgroup, factionalism and personal hatred must have been engendered by the events of the recent past that will take a generation to remove.

One could also surmise that the currents of anti-foreignism stirred up among at least some of the youth will not easily be contained. Has Chinese exclusiveness, so manifest in terms of overseas students and diplomatic practices even in Bandung days, been given a powerful new lease on life? And how will that affect the Chinese drive for global proletarian leadership in the years ahead?

If these are the heavy debts incurred, however, there would also appear to be assets of considerable significance. First, recent Chinese foreign policy has in many respects been essentially a projection of domestic policy, and viewed from the standpoint of those supporting the Cultural Revolution, it has played an indispensable role in supporting that revolution, granting certain "excesses" and mistakes. The mobilization techniques cultivated so ardently in the domestic sphere had to have an outlet also in the foreign arena. In this manner, a consistency or symmetry was achieved, and the more primitive, anti-foreign elements in Chinese nationalism could be released in a period of deep emotional stress. Attitudes and actions in the foreign policy sphere could thus serve in some sense as a diversion from serious internal rifts, particularly among the more militant Red Guard types. And at the same time, the cloak of isolation could be used with increasing effectiveness to force an intense concentration upon the internal scene and blot from the public mind as much of the unpleasantness of China's global position as possible. To rekindle revolutionary fervor in Mao's terms, one needed a period of looking inward.

It was perhaps symbolic of the quasi-isolation, quasi-involvement, characterizing Chinese foreign policy, however, that whereas foreign aid, foreign students, and diplomatic relations were all drastically curtailed, as we have noted, Chinese Communist external broadcasting continued to increase through the end of 1966 at least, with propaganda being sent to all parts of the world in 33 languages for a total of 1,103 hours per week.[31] Copies of Mao's collected works and of the little red book were turned out by the millions. According to official sources, in 1967 some 86,400,000 sets of Mao's selected works were printed, together with 350,000,000 copies of Mao's Quotations, 47,500,000 copies of his selected readings, and over 57,000,000 copies of his poems. "The radiance of his writings now shines everywhere, from the embattled jungles in Southeast Asia to the rugged Andes regions in South America, from the southern tip of Africa to Iceland near the Arctic Circle. Clearly, the sun never sets on the word of Mao!"[32]

Could anything illustrate more graphically the deeply ambivalent

character of Chinese foreign policy? As we have noted, such ambivalence is in no sense a new phenomena. Throughout Chinese history,
the principle of contradiction, the constant interaction of opposites, has
lain at the root of Chinese philosophy. In this respect as in certain
others, Mao is in the mainstream of Chinese tradition. New ideological,
technical, and inter-cultural inputs, to be sure, have drastically altered
certain practices and potentialities of the present. Nevertheless, an
understanding of Chinese foreign policy today--its style, central thrust,
and innate paradoxes--requires an appreciation of those twin forces of
exclusiveness and universalism that continue to coexist in an uneasy
relation within its folds. Constantly changing in form and relative weight,
these forces help to provide a central explanation for the seemingly in-
consistent, mercurial foreign policy of Communist China. In their further development and interaction, moreover, they will determine the
crucial question of whether it is to be peace or war in Asia.

Footnotes

1. For an early effort in the direction of suggesting that the Chinese revolutionary model was both applicable and available for other parts of Asia, see the speech by Liu Shao-ch'i at the Conference on Trade Unions of Asia and Oceania in Cominform Journal, For a Lasting Peace, For People's Democracy, December 30, 1949, p. 2.

2. For some estimates, see Hearings before the Joint Senate Committee on Armed Services and Foreign Relations, 82nd Congress, 1st Session, USGPO, Washington, 1951.
    For an insightful recent study of the Chinese military record in Korea, see Alexander L. George, The Chinese Communist Army in Action -- The Korean War and Its Aftermath, Columbia University Press, New York and London, 1967.

3. See Alice Langley Hsieh, Communist China's Strategy in the Nuclear Era, Prentice-Hall, Englewood Cliffs, New Jersey, 1962; Morton H. Halperin and Dwight H. Perkins, Communist China and Arms Control, East Asian Research Center, Harvard University, Cambridge, Massachusetts, 1965; and Ellis Joffe, "The Conflict between Old and New in the Chinese Army," in Roderick MacFarquhar (ed.), China Under Mao: Politics Takes Command, The M.I.T. Press, Cambridge (Mass,) and London, 1966, pp. 34-56.

4. For one interesting and detailed analysis of P'eng's dismissal, see David A. Charles, "The Dismissal of Marshal P'eng Teh-huai," in ibid., pp. 20-33.

5. See Hsieh, op. cit., p. 169.

6. See Peking Review, No. 33, August 16, 1963, p. 14.

7. "Counter-Revolutionary Revisionist Line in National Defense Research Repudiated," Peking Review, No. 37, September 8, 1967, pp. 9-11.
    See also "Peng Teh-huai and His Behind-the-Scenes Boss Cannot Shirk Responsibility for Their Crimes," a Jen-min Jih-pao editorial of August 25, 1967 in Peking Review, No. 35, August 25, 1967, pp. 6-7 (see also pp. 8-9); Li Hsin-kung, "Settle Accounts with Peng Teh-huai for His Heinous Crimes of Usurping Army Leadership and Opposing the Party," Peking Review, No. 36, September 1, 1967, pp. 12-15; and Excerpts from "Resolution of 8th Plenary Session of 8th Central Committee of CPC Concerning the Anti-Party Clique Headed by Peng Teh-

huai," August 16, 1959, in Peking Review, No. 34, August 18, 1967,
pp. 8-10.

8. See my "The Sino-Soviet Conflict in Perspective," The Annals of
the American Academy of Political and Social Science, Vol. 351, January 1964, pp. 1-14.

9. For a recent survey of Mao's thought on the subject of People's War,
see "Chairman Mao Tse-tung on People's War," Peking Review, August
4, 1967, pp. 5-13.

Among the other quotations were these: "Every Communist must
grasp the truth, 'Political power grows out of the barrel of a gun.'"

"According to the Marxist theory of the state, the army is the chief
component of state power. Whoever wants to seize and retain state
power must have a strong army. Some people ridicule us as advocates
of the 'omnipotence of war.' Yes, we are advocates of the omnipotence
of revolutionary war; that is good, not bad, it is Marxist. The guns
of the Russian Communist Party created socialism. We shall create a
democratic republic. Experience in the class struggle in the era of
imperialism teaches us that it is only by the power of the gun that the
working class and the labouring masses can defeat the armed bourgeoisie
and landlords; in this sense we may say that only with guns can the whole
world be transformed." (These quotations were taken from a speech entitled "Problems of War and Strategy," November 6, 1938, in Mao's
Selected Works, Vol. II, pp. 224-225.

10. Typical of the eulogies carried in the Chinese press is the following:
"The world has entered a new revolutionary era, one which has Mao Tse-
tung's thought as its great banner. It is an era when all revolutionaries
look to the red sun that rises in the East; their hearts turn to the greatest
leader of the people of the world, Chairman Mao. They hope day and
night that they can visit China--centre of the world revolution today and
see the great teacher of the world revolution. From the bottom of their
hearts, people sing his praises and sing in praise of Mao Tse-tung's
thought. They say that the invincible thought of Mao Tse-tung is the very
soul of the revolutionary people of the world!.........

"Chairman Mao, you are the great savior of mankind!
"Chairman Mao, you are the greatest Marxist-Leninist
of our time!
"Chairman Mao, you are the beacon for the people
of the world!
"Chairman Mao, we will always follow you in making
revolution, in striving for the emancipation of the

people of the whole world!"
"Mao Tse-tung's Thought Lights the Whole World," Peking Review,
No. 1, January 3, 1968, p. 37.

11. Ch'en Yi's remarks quoted here were made at a press conference
in Peking on September 29, 1965, and have been reported in slightly
different versions from various sources. The official version can be
found in the Peking Review, October 8, 1965.

12. In early 1968, General Huang was named Chairman of the Kwangtung Provincial Revolutionary Committee. Since this paper was written,
it has been reported that Huang has been elevated to the position of acting
Chief of Staff, and has now become "a leading comrade" of the Central
Committee, the Cultural Revolution group,and the Military Commission.
It would thus appear that Huang at this point is at least temporarily close
to the center of national power.

For a general analysis of great interest, see Chalmers Johnson,
"Lin Piao's Army and its Role in Chinese Society," Current Scene, Part
I, July 1, 1966,and Part II, July 15, 1966; and Ralph L. Powell, "Maoist
Military Doctrines," Asian Survey, Vol. VIII, No. 4, April 1968, pp.
239-262.

13. For estimates of Chinese aid through 1964, see Table E-1 and E-2
in Alexander Eckstein, Communist China's Economic Growth and Foreign
Trade, McGraw-Hill, New York-Toronto-London, 1966, pp. 306-307.
Eckstein believes that up to the end of 1964, China had committed close
to $2 billion in foreign aid, with somewhat more than $1 billion having
been used, the great bulk of it going to North Korea, North Vietnam,
Mongolia, Albania, and Hungary. p. 161.

14. The remaining 1,000 foreign students reportedly included 300 Afri-
cans (approximately 170 on academic courses), 125 Asians, 100 Albanians,
40 Mongolians, and 30 Middle Easterners.

15. For the Chinese notes to the Ceylon Government of August 19 and
23, see Communist China Digest, No. 190, October 16, 1967, pp. 12-13
and 15.

16. On August 22, 1967, the Chinese Embassy in Nairobi had delivered
a violent protest to the Kenya government alleging that Vice President
D.A. Moi had trumped up charges of illegal activities by Embassy officials. Asserting that the Kenyan government was working "energetically
in the service of U.S. imperialism in plotting the 'two China's' scheme,"

the protest note went on to state: "The Chinese absolutely will not tolerate such blatant interference in China's internal affairs and your flagrant hostility toward the Chinese people...." Ibid. , p. 14.

17. Jiji Poll, Tokyo, Japan, September 1967. It is interesting to note that Communist China took over the cellar spot in popularity from the Soviet Union beginning in August 1966, the month of the famous 11th Plenum and a period marked by the beginning of large-scale Red Guard activities.

18. A spokesman in the Ministry of Foreign Affairs was reported to have told the Mongolian Ambassador in February 1967, that diplomatic immunity was a remnant of bourgeois institutions and a country carrying out a revolution could not recognize bourgeois norms.

19. See Communist China Digest, No. 190, October 16, 1967, pp. 11-12.

20. See Ibid. , No. 191, October 31, 1967, pp. 42-43.

21. Ibid. , No. 192, November 24, 1967, pp. 39-41.

22. The text of Ch'en Yi's self-criticism may be found in Hung Wei Pao, (The Red Guard paper), of the Peking Foreign Languages Institute, dated February 8, 1967, and entitled, "Wo te Chien-ch'a, (My Self-Criticism)."

23. For two major attacks upon Ch'en during this period, see "P'ao ta Ch'en Yi, Chieh Fang Wai Shih K'ou (Bombard Ch'en Yi, Liberate Foreign Affairs Circles)," signed by the Red First Company of the Red Flag of Peking, and published in Hung Ch'i, April 4, 1967; and "Ch'en Yi Ho Ch'i Tu Yeh (How Poisonous Ch'en Yi Is)," in Hung Wei Chan P'ao (Red Guard Combat Paper), of the Red Guard of the People's University of China, April 13, 1967.

24. Storm, a Red Guard Newspaper dated November 26, 1967.

25. See "Tui Wang Ping te Liu Tien Huai Yi (Six Points of Doubt Concerning Wang Ping)," signed by the People's Combat Team of the Foreign Languages Press, and published in Hung Wei Pao, dated February 8, 1967.

26. It is interesting to note that the Peking Review of August 25, 1967, featured a picture of Yao Wen-yuan seated with Mao Tse-tung when Mao

received Vangjel Moisiu and Myfit Mushi, two Albanian "experts" working in China. Yao was described as a "member of the Cultural Revolution Group Under the Central Committee of the Chinese Communist Party and head of the Chinese Red Guard Delegation which attended the Fifth Congress of the Albanian Union of Working Youth. " p. 5.

27. In addition to the materials cited above, see "Thoroughly Smash the Privileged Stratum in the Ministry of Foreign Affairs," in Wai-shih Hung-ch'i, June 14, 1967, attributed to the Red Guards Service Center of Returned Students of the Capital Red Guard Congress, and translated in full in Communist China Digest, No. 190, October 16, 1967, pp. 112-117.

28. For two general attacks upon the so-called Liu-Teng foreign policy line, see Yen Chang-Kwei, "Bourgeois Counter-Revolutionary Strategy and Tactics," Peking Review, No. 52, December 25, 1967, pp. 34-40, which represents an abridged translation of the original article in Chieh-fang Chun-pao, November 13, 1967; and "Our Banner is the Great Chinese Communist Party, Our Great Leader Chairman Mao--The Quest of Strategy and Tactics in the Chinese Revolution, a Big Poisonous Weed, Wrathfully Denounced at a Rally of Proletarian Revolutionaries of the Army," Jen-min Jih-pao, October 13, 1967, translated in Communist China Digest, No. 193, January 8, 1968, pp. 54-63.

29. "Ch'en Yi Ho Ch'i Tu Yeh," (See footnote 23).

30. For many months, the Peking Review has carried a section entitled, "Mao Tse-tung's Thought Lights the Whole World," (See footnote 10).

31. Broadcasting in 33 languages, the Chinese in 1966 beamed 415 hours per week to the Far East (300 of these to Taiwan), 281 hours to South and Southeast Asia, 190 to Europe and 105 to Black Africa. Transmissions to Latin America totalled 42 hours per week, to North America 63 hours, and to the Middle East and North Africa, 42 hours.

32. Peking Review, No. 1, January 3, 1968, pp. 14-15.

THE STRUCTURE OF CONFLICT: CHINA IN 1967

Ezra F. Vogel

Whatever hardships the events of 1967 brought to China, they have provided new information and insights to scholars trying to understand the dynamics of Chinese politics. Never before had the Communist Party and the state been subjected to such attack. Never before were internal political tensions revealed so openly. Accounts of these discussions have reached the West from many sources, including Red Guard newspapers, reports of wall posters, observations of foreign visitors, reports by refugees, and official communist newspapers, magazines, and radio broadcasts. Used with discretion, these materials permit a more detailed analysis of internal political conflicts than has heretofore been possible. This paper will attempt to interpret from these diverse sources the structure of social and political cleavages in 1967.

The Heightening of Political Cleavages

The history of the Chinese Communist movement is filled with internal disagreements, "rectifications," purges, and reorganizations. In the period after World War II, however, the war against the KMT and the subsequent excitement of victory created a strong sense of patriotic solidarity in which members of various persuasions and factions subordinated their own interests to the national good. From 1945 to 1959 only one major Party figure, Kao Kang, was purged.

No revolution can long sustain an élan in which local interests, based on historical and cultural differences, are sacrificed for the total good. The hopes for modernization aroused during the revolution began to fade as local political leaders realized the magnitude of the effort required to overcome China's backwardness. Even without policy errors, it was inevitable that cleavages temporarily under control at the time of "Liberation" would re-emerge when the revolutionary élan and optimism were no longer strong enough to contain the divisive tendencies.

The inevitable erosion of revolutionary élan was hastened by disagreements over three major issues. In each case Chairman Mao pushed through a decision despite considerable resistance. When the decisions led to serious problems the resistance hardened, and basic political cleavages became more severe. These issues were: (1) the speed of collectivization, (2) the extent of mass mobilization in 1957-1958, and (3) the degree of independence from the Soviet Union.

In 1955, discarding the plans of Party bureaucrats, Mao suddenly decided to speed up collectivization. By early 1956, as implementation difficulties became apparent, the Soviet Union denounced Stalin, who had also trampled over opposition in pushing through rapid collectivization. Needless to say, this encouraged Mao's critics, who led an attack on the cult of personality at the Eighth Party Congress.

Mao's decision to widen the rift with the Soviet Union encouraged further opposition based on fears that China would have to confront the United States without the Soviet shield, and that she would be deprived of Soviet aid for building a modern army and industrial system.

Nothing did more to erode revolutionary esprit or harden the opposition than the failure of the Great Leap Forward. Many Party leaders, convinced that Mao's romantic and arbitrary utopianism was dangerous for the country, became more determined in their opposition. They united in tempering utopianism at the Sixth Plenum in December, 1958, in backing Peng Teh-huai in the summer of 1959, and in forcing the retrenchment at the Ninth Plenum in early 1961. Even if the opposition did not actually attempt a coup in early 1962, Mao was removed from the presidency of the Government in 1959 and his day-to-day control over Party affairs was restricted.

The Great Proletarian Cultural Revolution of 1967 is therefore merely the culmination of a longstanding conflict between Mao and his opposition. It is now clear that, with army help, Mao fought to regain power within his Party apparatus at least as early as September, 1962. However, with serious food shortages and opposition to the Great Leap Forward at its height, he was unable to mount a strong counterattack. Early in 1964 Mao began using the army's propaganda and organizational apparatus to penetrate political, economic, and educational organizations. By late 1965, the national economy had revived, the United States had made it clear that it would not attack China unless China sent troops to Vietnam, and the Chinese Army had a strong power base in civilian organizations. Mao then launched his attack to regain control over the Party and government apparatus.

The Nature of Factions

During the period of the United Front and during the early consolidation of state power, intellectuals, businessmen, and other prominent citizens were granted considerable influence because of their critical role in rallying popular support for the government. Although their role gradually declined, the Hundred Flowers Campaign was a recognition of their continued importance. However, by mid-1957, the influence of non-Party members was severely restricted because by then the concentration of power in the Party, Government, and army was more complete and more openly acknowledged. Opposition, to be effective, had to take place from within the state, Party, and army apparatus. While the state bureaucracy, in fact has a considerable role in economic planning and resource allocation, basic policy questions of public security, education, and cultural affairs are inevitably discussed and decided within the Party. The Party exercises critical power at every level through the Party committee, the secretariat, and the organization department.

Over the years, the membership of any given Party committee, including the secretariat and the organization department, tended to solidify and members who did not fit in with the dominant leadership were replaced. In addition to the ordinary opportunities for transferring dissident elements, officials could use rectification campaigns to remove opponents. Since the highest leaders at any given level are appointed by the secretariat and the organization department of the next level, there tends to be some linkage between levels within the Party hierarchy. The Maoists' characterization of their opponents as members of "cliques," "gangs," and "dens" undoubtedly refers to this tendency toward solidification within Party committees and the linkages between Party levels.

The factions in the Chinese Communist Party are by no means closed factions, for their membership is heterogeneous and changing. This contrasts with factions in warlord China, which were built up almost entirely by one man, and with the university factions within the Japanese bureaucracy which are essentially closed ascriptive membership groups. Those who wield power in the Party at any given level are not only from different localities, but they have served in various units of the army, and have worked under various leaders. Because so many decisions involving serious consequences for bureaucrats and their localities had to be made, many policy differences arose among leaders at any given level. Even within a Party committee, most secretaries represent specific organizational interests which frequently conflict.

The various secretaries may in turn be responsible for such diverse sector organizations as public security, agriculture, military, labor work, industry, propaganda, education, and culture. Also the leaders at any given level are differentially concerned with the various geographical subdivisions within their jurisdiction. Furthermore, higher level Party bureaucrats follow the traditional Chinese bureaucratic practice of cultivating heterogeneity at lower levels in order to prevent the consolidation of interest groups which would be less responsive to control.

Because of this heterogeneity and flux within the organization, a Party committee cannot assume that all its members will remain loyal under all circumstances. Thus, as in the case of some warlord alliances in pre-Communist China, it is possible that a leader in one faction can with due compensation be enticed to desert to another faction. The essence of political rectification strategy is to split the opposition. It is the attempt of some factions to recruit members from other factions that provides so much of the fluidity in the Cultural Revolution.

The Party also has the problem of a generation gap. Younger officials are increasingly educated and oriented to bureaucratic structures while most of the Party elite, at all levels, are the product of a quite different experience. They grew up in an unsettled period in which talented young men sought not training and skills but heroism and glory. They are self-made revolutionaries who fought against the Japanese or the Kuomintang. Given the character of guerrilla war, they often operated with considerable independence in local areas for extended periods of time and as a result their style of leadership is proud and personalistic. They still strive for glory and honor. Despite the attempts to institute democratic discussions into the Party structure, they still expect and ordinarily receive unquestioned compliance from their subordinates. Thus, even with systematic party-building, it is not easy for the top leaders to secure the cooperation of the proud self-made men below them. When conflict arises there is always the danger that those who have suffered indignities will, if given the opportunity, seek revenge and "settle accounts."

As in political parties in non-communist countries, the Chinese Communist Party is an amalgam of diverse interests. During the last several years the struggle has been increasingly polarized between the Maoists and the Party bureaucrats. In the same way as it is difficult for nations to remain unaligned in the presence of two large super-powers, so, too, it is difficult for power-holders within China to remain unaligned in the struggle between Party bureaucrats and the Maoists.

The leading Party bureaucrats derive their power through the Party Secretariat and the organization department. In recent years they have formed an impressive alliance including most of those on the Central Committee Politburo, most Party leaders in the regional bureaus, and, through them, the leaders at the provincial, special district, municipal, and county levels. Also included are most of the members of the Secretariat and most of the leading Party secretaries in the central government, the regions, the provinces, the special districts, the counties, and the cities. Their influence extends into the government bureaucracy, especially in the public security and propaganda spheres, though they have left control over some of the more technical and specialized branches of government to administrative specialists. Although they are relatively weak in the military, the ties between regional and provincial Party leaders on the one hand and the regional and district military leaders on the other and the tie between the Party and the political department of the army have also given them considerable influence in certain army circles.

As power polarized, the Maoists built their support around a small group of loyal propagandists such as Ch'en Po-ta and Chiang Ch'ing and the dominant group in the army led by Lin Piao. With these groups as a core, the Maoists formed a somewhat uneasy alliance with certain government bureaucrats like Chou En-lai and Hsieh Fu-chih. Some of these army leaders and government bureaucrats also have considerable power within the Party. In addition, some Party leaders, either out of personal loyalty or because of old enmities with the dominant Party machine, have chosen to side with Mao.

It is not possible on the basis of available evidence to distinguish precisely which individual has taken what stand at every major turning point of the last several years. Nevertheless on the basis of revelations of the Red Guard period it is possible to distinguish fundamental differences of policy and approach which have separated the Party bureaucrats from the Maoists. The Party bureaucrats have been fundamentally concerned with regularizing Party and government machinery and in concentrating on production. They are convinced that China will become stronger by developing specialized skills in the Party, government, and the economic and educational spheres. Although accepting the notion that politics should be in command, they believe that it is dangerous to interfere with the regular processes of production through mass mobilization campaigns. They are convinced that excessive optimism, uncoordinated and unplanned assaults on production, and emphasis on sheer willpower can be dangerous, as was the case in the Great Leap Forward. Although staunch nationalists, they are more prepared to work within the framework of the international communist movement and to make more concessions to Russia in exchange for the nuclear umbrella and technical assistance.

Just as American and British leaders are preoccupied with their experience at Munich and as the Japanese leaders are preoccupied with the nightmare of militarism, the Chinese Maoists are preoccupied with a vision from their past--the vision of the moral degeneration of a bureaucracy which is out of touch with the people, the core problem which led to the decline and fall of the Kuomintang.

Concerned with the decline of enthusiasm which was especially marked after collectivization, the Maoists have tried to revitalize the revolutionary spirit of the people through mass mobilization campaigns and by forcing Party and government cadres to give up their offices and specialized work to live and work among the masses under the same adverse circumstances in which poor Chinese peasants work. Realizing that China is essentially a backward agrarian economy, the Maoists are convinced that at least in the short run it is the enthusiasm of the masses which is crucial in increasing overall production. They are willing to push mass mobilization even if it temporarily interferes with production. Convinced that the attitude of the broad masses is critical, they side with the poorer peasants against the richer ones and with poorer students against those who come from better prepared "bourgeois" backgrounds. Although desirous of building a strong modern army, the Maoists are reluctant to make concessions to those who insist that modern weaponry is basic for a strong army. Instead, the Maoists place greater stress than do their opponents on the militia, on the guerrillas, and on revolutionary warfare as a means of expanding China's power and preventing invasion.

Although the roots of power are by no means simple, in general the Party bureaucrats have relied on organizational discipline and the personal ties among their members. They are political craftsmen who make use of the techniques of skilled politicians everywhere. The Maoists rely essentially on a combination of propaganda and mass mobilization, with a solid underpinning of military support.

Strategies

Maoist Strategy. The essential problem of Maoist strategy during the Great Proletarian Cultural Revolution has been how to purge large numbers of Party leaders without going through regular Party channels. Although Mao made use of the Central Committee Plenum in August 1966 to attack his opposition, it is apparent even from statements made by his wife that he represented only a minority of the Central Committee. He pushed through the basic program of the Cultural Revolution only by stacking the meetings with sympathetic young activists and mounting large demonstrations of military power. At the lower levels, the Party bureaucrats were so well unified that it was not even possible to use Party channels for the carrying out of purges. A new ad hoc Cultural Revolution group with a hierarchy at all levels and new mass organizations of students, employees, workers, and peasants had to be established. Although we lack sufficient information about the structure of this organization, it appears to have been built largely around the army and the militia, with heavy reliance on personal connections. With this as a core the Maoists were able to recruit into their mass organization government cadres, many Party bureaucrats, many workers, some peasants, and especially students.

Unlike the strategy in Stalin's purges, the objective of the Maoist purge is not simply to remove the opposition. From the beginning, Chinese Communist leaders of all persuasions have been concerned with the attitudes of the masses and it is this concern which has kept them from imprisoning or killing their opponents. Instead, the goal is the mobilization of opinion so that the masses come to view a purge as necessary and right. In the case of the land reform program, for example, the aim was not simply to redistribute the landlords' land, but to discredit the landlords so thoroughly that they could never rally support and effectively resist the Party's policies. In order to consolidate mass opinion, it is desirable that the guilty confess to the charges against him. If he is well know and popular, he is treated well to prevent his followers from solidifying their opposition. Obviously, in attacking so many opponents, the Maoists have not been able to carry out this process to perfection. The slowness of the process derives from the difficulty of building sufficient political support and enthusiasm among the masses for removing the opposition.

The task of constructing a new ad hoc organization for attacking the Party bureaucrats has been a formidable one, even with a core of the army and militia. Because the Party bureaucrats are political organizers par excellence, the ad hoc organizations have difficulty in matching their organizational skills. In expanding to a national scale, an ad hoc cultural revolutionary structure has difficulty remaining free of influence by opposition Party leaders. Therefore, cultural revolutionary committees have not been able to move with the precision, planning, and accuracy of a strictly military or secret police organization.

Because Maoist strategy aims to rouse the masses and to enlist them in the cause, control over the mass media was of primary importance. Mao himself noted during the Cultural Revolution that one must first carry on propaganda work. At the outset, the Party propaganda network was untrustworthy and therefore, in the spring of 1966, the Maoists moved to bring it under control. The army propaganda machine took the lead, working through the existing papers and radio networks, and supplemented by "revolutionary masses" and the Red Guard papers and posters.

Reliance on young intellectuals to carry the message to the masses is in keeping with Chinese practices dating back to the turn of the century. Young intellectuals had been a driving force in Sun Yat-sen's revolutionary movement, in Kuomintang nationalism, in anti-Japanese resistance, and in the founding of the Communist state. They have remained the most politicized and devoted segment of the population and the most effective mobilizers of the masses.

However, for a variety of reasons, not all youth were devoted Maoists. When the Cultural Revolution attacked representatives of the bourgeois class, students from bourgeois backgrounds could have few illusions about their own vulnerability. The frequency with which they were told that class characteristics were not necessarily inherited, i. e. , that they were not subject to attack simply because of their backgrounds, reveals their lingering suspicion. Children of Party and state cadres were heavily represented in the student population, and even though many of them were excluded from Red Guard organizations, they had friends in them. Accounts of Red Guard organizations which have reached the West make it clear that they included many "impure elements", but even if these were weeded out students were no match for the well-disciplined Party and army leaders. Their training and experience had taught the wisdom of following Party leaders. Furthermore, many were cautious in attacking leaders who might yet have opportunities for revenge. The Red Guard movement also appealed to some as a means of advancing their careers, and the resulting competition introduced another element of conflict.

The army was by far the most disciplined and responsive Maoist instrument, and in the power showdown its support was crucial. The army was not wholly united, however, and disunity reached a peak when it was criticized by "ultra leftists." Lin Piao is known to have some opposition within the army, especially among some old revolutionary heroes and among associates and followers of former Marshall P'eng Teh-huai. Many military leaders were reluctant to become so heavily involved in internal political tasks at the expense of their military responsibilities. Even if the military leaders were thoroughly committed to Mao, the Maoists wished to give the impression of massive popular support. Because the use of troops scarcely contributed to that image, the army was used as a last resort. Even when the army became involved, it was so small that it had to rely on the militia, especially in rural areas, but it was difficult to keep the militia entirely free of Party influence.

The basic dilemma confronting the Maoists throughout the Cultural Revolution has been to press the campaign just hard enough to remove the Party power holders without overextending themselves by stirring up more opposition than can be successfully controlled. The campaign took place in a series of waves. In each wave, the Maoists expanded the scope or severity of attacks, and after each attack moved to isolate the purgees from their supporters. When disorder was too serious, the Maoists would slow down the pace of attack. When the strength of the opposition seemed to be a more serious problem than the extent of disorders, the Maoists again expanded their attacks.

One way of reducing the severity of the disorders was to prohibit or restrict the use of weapons. In the fall of 1967, for example, they systematically collected weapons to de-escalate the conflicts. Although guns were in fact used at times, many of the conflicts were limited to picks, clubs, stones, chairs, and other implements which the Red Guards could use in their hand-to-hand struggles. The Maoists could also de-escalate the conflict by curtailing wall posters, narrowing the scope of attack, and assuring potential purgees that only a few of them were vulnerable to attack.

Except for the all-out attack on the opposition in early 1967, the Maoists have been successful in isolating the purgees and attacking the opposition bit by bit. As in other political rectification campaigns, they commonly attacked some lesser figure than the main target, both to warn the main target in hopes of gaining his backing and to reduce his base of support in case it became necessary to attack him directly. In retrospect, for example, it appears that Yang Hsien-cheng was attacked in 1964 to warn the highest level Party bureaucrats. Once a leader is exposed, the Maoists try to destroy his base of support completely, or if he is a "wavering element," to extract a confession and bring his followers firmly behind the "revolutionaries." The Red Guard press and the Red Guard posters played a critical role in warning an official without escalating the criticism to the official level and, if he were stubborn, in reducing his base of support in preparation for formal attacks. Only when the informal Red Guard criticism reached a certain level was the purgee mentioned by name in the official press, and the top two opponents, Liu Shao-ch'i and Teng Hsiao-p'ing, are still referred to in the official press only as "China's Khruschev" and "the other leading person taking the capitalist road."

Within limits, the Maoists could regulate the severity of attacks against possible opposition. When the attack was severe, they would completely expose the target's personal background, including his childhood and family history. In a milder attack, the emphasis was on recent errors, especially the errors made during the course of the Cultural Revolution. For example, T'ao Chu was attacked thoroughly for all his "bourgeois" predilections, errors of decades ago, and his family background. Yeh Chien-ying, however, was subjected to a lesser attack and was criticized only for his most recent errors. If the attack were severe the victim was criticized for his fundamental character and class outlook, but if it were less severe he would be described as basically good but misguided or misled.

Anti-Maoist Strategy. In general, the anti-Maoists have not had enough power and legitimation to attack directly. No official newspaper, radio station, or other formal media has directly criticized Chairman Mao. Some of the media have at times resisted Maoist pressures to publish articles and some have even published veiled attacks on lesser Maoists. However, the opposition has not been strong enough to mount a systematic attack on such major opponents as Ch'en Po-ta or Chiang Ch'ing. Lacking control over official and public media, they have had to carry on their propaganda work through personal and sometimes clandestine channels. In general the anti-Maoists have found it more effective to hide under the Maoist cover. They "fight the Red Flag by waving the Red Flag."

Much of the strategy of the anti-Maoists is simply defensive. They protect their personnel records, they hide or burn archives and other evidence which might incriminate them. They warn their fellows of impending attacks, they physically remove themselves from certain areas, and they confuse the opposition with smokescreens. They confess when pressed, but they avoid supplying information or clues which might be used against them.

In some cases the anti-Maoists have waged a form of guerrilla war by encouraging strikes among workers, disrupting industrial work, and sabotaging communication and transport facilities. In cases where they had some military support, they have engaged in small-scale military confrontations. Some have even retreated to rural or mountainous areas to escape being attacked.

The most widespread and effective methods of resistance have been organizational and propaganda sabotage. By stirring up workers or peasants they "hoodwink the masses" into resisting the encroachment of Red Guards and Revolutionary rebels. Students could use Maoist slogans while encouraging certain Red Guard groups to resist or attack other Red Guard groups. It was especially easy to stir up local Red Guards to resist outside Red Guards. Anti-Maoists could work from within Maoist mass organizations to create confusion and obfuscate issues, or to press for attacks so broad as to stiffen the opposition. Those who occupied important and strategic positions in schools, factories, or transportation networks could simply be absent from work, causing production difficulties. Taking advantage of the self interest of local peasant and worker groups they could, for example, encourage industrial workers to request higher wages or bonuses or retain their produce. Red Guard groups could be encouraged to pursue their own interests in opposition to other groups. In short, although they lacked the force to win clear-cut victories, the veteran Party bureaucrats had, through indirect and subtle means, the ability to slow down and sabotage the Proletarian Cultural Revolution.

"Waverers." The vast mass of the citizenry is less committed to one side or the other than to ending up on the winning side. Many, impressed in the past with the capacity of the Party to end up on top in any dispute, were inclined in the early confusion to bet on the Party leaders as the eventual victors. By the beginning of 1967, most were betting on the Maoist revolutionaries. Whichever side they were betting on, most hedged their bets, expressing the minimal support necessary to get by at any given time while not arousing the opposition any more than necessary.

During the course of the Cultural Revolution, many ordinary cadres and citizens found ample reason to become annoyed at the brash young "revolutionaries." Many workers, for example, disliked the intrusion of militant and somewhat undisciplined student groups into their place of work or residence. Local citizens and even local Red Guards have resented the intrusions and the cockiness of "revolutionaries" from other areas. When peasants living along major transport routes or in the suburbs of urban areas were forced to share their quotas or quarters with visiting Red Guards or with lawless elements scarcely distinguishable from Red Guards or ex-Red Guards, many lost their enthusiasm for the revolution. Many of these local groups of workers, farmers, and ordinary urban residents have banded together in para-military organizations to defend themselves against intrusions from whatever outsiders.

However, the pressures for commitment are difficult to avoid and, once made, they are not easy to change. If a commitment involved a high degree of activism, even confession and official pardon would not free one from suspicion. Although cadres and ordinary citizens are often encouraged to believe that they will be welcomed by new power groups if they will only renounce their former allegiances, they realize that they are in a highly vulnerable position. When those who have made a serious commitment to a given faction find themselves under attack, they know there is often little likelihood that they will be forgiven by the opposition and they correctly perceive that the only alternative is to fight on with whatever means they have. Some of the most serious conflicts arise in this context, i.e., those who made firm commitments have no choice but to fight on to defend themselves.

Soldiers. Soldiers are not so numerous or sufficiently skilled in political organizational work that they can become involved in the day-to-day political struggle. However, by and large they retain a very deep and almost sacred dedication to the army and to China. When they are brought into the Cultural Revolution, their basic task is to keep order. Since they are considered responsible for keeping order, it is under-standable that even when told to support revolutionaries they should discipline those creating disorder as much as the Party bureaucrats de-fending the status quo. Even though willing to support Chairman Mao, many army leaders were not willing to go along with the most militant Red Guards and revolutionary rebels, especially when they invaded army compounds to obtain weapons, to criticize or discredit army personnel, or to press the army to take a stronger stand in favor of revolutionaries. Army leaders were notably unenthusiastic about such encroachments and by late summer 1967, when chaos reached new heights, they were able to get a clear mandate that revolutionaries should stay away, a mandate that must have been the envy of many civilians.

Because there are not enough soldiers with adequate understanding of local political situations, the role of keeping peace between various militant factions has taxed local army leaders beyond their capacity. Many local army groups, in their early peace-keeping efforts, were inclined to work closely with the dominant and relatively most cooperative faction. This sometimes roused the opposition to stir up trouble to prevent stabilization until their faction was better represented. During much of the Cultural Revolution the army was told to keep peace without using weapons or resorting to violence. Although this limited escalation of the conflict, the result was not an absence of struggle but an intensification of small-scale conflicts and fighting. The degree of factionalism generated by the Cultural Revolution made it very difficult for the army to succeed in its basic task of keeping order, whether the local military allied with a given faction or tried to form a coalition government.

Organization Under Stress

After the Communists split with the Nationalists in 1927, their survival depended on keeping their organization free of spies. Through constant mutual discussion, examination, and criticism, they maintained a relatively pure, responsive, and disciplined organization. Even with the growth of political organizations after 1949, the Party maintained a careful check on new recruits to ensure loyalty and discipline.

The leaders of the Cultural Revolution could not possibly build up a new organization with comparable discipline. Although directives from Peking specified that reliable Party committees could be used to carry out the Cultural Revolution, there is no evidence that any major Party committee was found to be sufficiently loyal. Even if the militia or some other organization could provide the backbone for revolutionary mass organizations, these new structures had so many new responsibilities and so many new members that they were full of inconsistencies, stops and starts, and changes of direction. They were riddled with conflict not only over the content of decisions, but even over procedures for making decisions. In early 1967, for example, the Paris Commune model of mass democracy and open elections was trumpeted with great verve, but within weeks this theme was abandoned and replaced by calls for better discipline.

To coordinate the fast-moving actions of new members, the leaders of revolutionary organizations had no choice but to rely on incessant meetings. The long and late night meetings of the very highest leadership indicate the degree to which these organizations were dependent on a few leaders for decisions.

One of the most critical problems was the resolution of disputes between competing factions. In the fast-moving factional in-fighting in any locality, it was not always possible to wait for directives from above. As in the period of guerrilla warfare, it was necessary to allow local groups considerable initiative in choosing targets and responding to attacks. Although there was constant contact between levels through telegram, telephone, and visits, the communication was imperfect and at higher levels leaders were sometimes reluctant to make decisions too quickly. The imperfections in communications made it possible for local factions to manipulate higher levels through biased reporting and personal contacts, and to manipulate rival factions by "fake" telegrams and directives which they claimed they received from higher levels. In the course of overcoming factional disputes, leaders of local revolutionary organizations poured into Peking to receive the blessings of the leadership.

Higher leaders had limited control over local factions. When a local faction refused to follow orders or subtly undermined orders from above, the higher level often lacked capacity to enforce its decisions. Therefore, early in the conflict, higher levels were often cautious in making decisions about local factions until they could test their relative power. Similarly local groups sometimes hedged their bets on the higher level group likely to emerge in power, and not infrequently the fear of making errors which could later be punished exceeded the fear of disobeying immediate orders.

Amidst the chaos and disorder, there was even the basic question of how organizations were to be legitimized. The foundation of the state was legitimized originally through the Common Program and the People's Consultative Conference, and the state Constitution later provided an additional symbol of legitimacy. The Party procedures, the Party Constitution, and even the Party itself had become accepted as legitimate bases of authority. When these bases were disrupted during the Cultural Revolution, there was need for a new principle of political legitimacy. By propagandizing the cult of Mao, the Maoists have succeeded in gaining widespread acceptance of the assumption that virtue and legitimacy originate in the correct carrying out of the Thoughts of Chairman Mao. The success of the Maoists in gaining acceptance of this assumption is reflected in the fact that even the opposition must claim fidelity to the Thoughts of Mao and sometimes even use names such as Maoist Principles as a title for their own group.

The new principle of Maoism as a basis of legitimacy is not always easy to apply in practice. When Mao or one of his recognized representatives has given clear and unquestioned approval to a certain group, this group acquires a basis of legitimation over its rivals. Amidst chaos, however, Maoist leaders cannot possibly make decisions on every local situation, and they cannot afford to make too many errors lest the group they select be relatively unpopular or undisciplined. As a result many local conflicts have continued for long periods without the central leadership granting specific approval to any one group. As a result, even when there was a valid basis for recognizing a local faction as Maoist, it would not be legitimized immediately.

The Course of the Conflict in 1967

The beginning of 1967 saw the opening of the largest wave of assaults on Party leadership in the entire Cultural Revolution. By mid-fall 1966, it was clear that the student revolutionaries, even with logistic support from the army, were unable to accomplish their original goals. As Lin Piao often put it, the basic question in a revolution is seizure of power. The Red Guards had not seized power, nor had they been able to pressure Party leaders to submit wholeheartedly to Maoist leadership. Despite the engaging appeals of Chairman Mao, in October 1966, Liu Shao-ch'i and others issued confessions too weak to cause his followers to submit to the Maoists. Certain "pawns" had been sacrificed, especially in the cultural sphere, but the leading Party secretaries remained.

By October 1966, some Maoists had begun to lauch small-scale attacks on Party leaders through wall posters and Red Guard newspapers. In December, the attack was expanded to a bold and direct assault on Party headquarters. Because Party leaders still had solid roots in the Party organizations in factories, public utilities, and transport and communication networks, potentially they could cause great damage to the economy as the Party headquarters were attacked. The Maoists therefore built up among cadres and workers new mass organizations of "revolutionary rebels," paralleling the Red Guards, in order to safeguard these organizations from sabotage and work layoffs. Since student Red Guards, no matter how revolutionary, were hardly a match for experienced and sometimes armed men, older and more experienced men, the "revolutionary rebels," were therefore organized to undertake this more difficult task. Charging that Party leaders had been wasting money, they moved to take over economic organizations in Shanghai and elsewhere where disruptions were becoming serious. With the collaboration of Red

Guards, they mobilized masses of men and youths to take over the head-quarters of Party and government organs throughout the country and gradually to establish new leadership groups to direct these organizations.

Until January 1967 the army had remained in the background, but the chaos created by "storming the headquarters" was so great that by late January the army was brought into the Cultural Revolution more directly and completely than ever before. Little information is available on what happened to the rank and file of cadres after their headquarters were attacked in January 1967. Many Party units had been so intimidated as early as mid-1966 that they had ceased to meet. Even though former Party members continued to have liaisons after the "takeover" in January, and even though some lower level Party organs were still functioning, the Party hierarchy had clearly lost its political effectiveness and was by-passed by the army. The government bureaucracy, however, did continue to function after the seizure of power, albeit with new leadership and with a certain degree of paralysis resulting from the ability to make important new decisions so soon after the seizure of power when even personnel questions had not been entirely resolved.

As the army began to move in, the role of young intellectuals was correspondingly decreased. Students who antagonized workers and cadres and resisted pressures for discipline were ordered to return home and "make revolution" in their own schools.

Upon seizing power the Maoists began encouraging the army and the revolutionary rebels to establish new political organs at the top level in each region, province, and major municipality. In several provinces and in Peking and Shanghai the leaders moved almost immediately to establish new "Revolutionary Committees." These were largely civilian and included former cadres and Party leaders who were willing to co-operate with the new leadership. These "Triple Alliances" of army leaders, revolutionaries and former cadres were formed only in these two cities and in a small number of provinces. It soon became apparent that the situation was not sufficiently stable in most of the country to make selection of new leadership possible. As a result power rested directly with the military forces, and the military in turn supervised the revolutionaries and cadres while postponing the attempt to combine some old cadres and new revolutionaries into a new civilian structure.

Under ordinary circumstances a fundamental maxim of purge strategy is not to attack too broad an area. One should isolate an opponent carefully before attacking him so that his supporters do not move into the opposition with him. Because of the fast pace of the Cultural

Revolution and the unity and strength of the opposition, the Maoists found it necessary to violate this maxim; they launched an attack that was breathtaking in its unprecedented scope. Consequently, the work of isolating the opposition, usually done before an attack, had to be accomplished after the fact.

Following the January-February takeovers, therefore, the Maoists attempted to isolate the purgees from the rank and file of cadres. Cadres were assured that the vast majority of cadres were all right. They had not made "errors" but simply had been misled by their Party and government leaders. Therefore if they but renounced their former leaders and confessed their errors, they would be welcomed into the fold under the new arrangements. The new leaders tried to reduce the scale of the attack, to prevent undisciplined attacks, and to prevent ordinary cadres from having undue anxiety that might cause them to collaborate with the opposition.

No matter how much the leaders tried to pull the cadres away from the "small number of persons in authority" under attack, they were not entirely successful. So many former Party leaders were attacked that they and their allies in the army were able to produce what the Maoists termed a "counter-current" in February and March. After the forceful attacks of January and February, the Party leaders could not oppose the Maoists directly. However, in the confusion and rapid expansion of revolutionary organizations, many were able to join them or at least influence other rebels and create confusion and disruption within the revolutionary ranks.

After the "takeovers" of January and February, the revolutionaries were clearly overextended. In the effort to establish order it was often necessary to make concessions to former cadres in order to make use of their knowledge. To preserve order it was necessary, as Chou En-lai and others directed, to clamp down on the less-disciplined revolutionaries even more than on the former cadres. Since military leaders could not always control all the subtle political maneuverings within the new organizations, the political in-fighting was often dominated by the old cadres who were more skilled in political craftsmanship.

By March many of the most militant leaders in the Maoist camp were discouraged by these conservative tendencies and tried to force the military leaders to give more support to the revolutionaries. Revolutionaries entered army compounds to obtain weapons, to search out opposition, and to prod the army into giving more support. The conflict became increasingly sharp between the revolutionaries trying to preserve their power in the new organizational structure and the army leaders trying to keep order. It was clear that both sides had the support of some higher leaders in Peking. By the end of March, however, the more militant Maoists were winning the day in Peking. In an effort to prevent army leaders from quelling the revolutionaries, the central authorities issued on April 6 a new ten-point directive reducing the power of the army and giving more support to the revolutionaries. In implementing this new swing to the left, military leaders who had worked to keep order were criticized severely for not sufficiently supporting the revolutionary organizations. Once criticized, the military leaders were anxious to avoid further errors and were therefore more cautious when they were again told to keep order.

Beginning in April, the limitations on peace-keeping operations and continued encouragement to revolutionaries led to chaos in many parts of the country. Sabotage to rail transportation and communications reached a new height, and clashes between groups of revolutionaries and between revolutionaries and Party bureaucrats reached new and more serious proportions. Army leaders, having undergone criticism before, remained largely on the sidelines despite directives to keep order. In some cases guns and other weapons were involved, but more commonly, the fights were between groups using sticks, stones, clubs, chairs, axes, and other implements.

By early August serious economic damage had been done and there was disaffection by many military leaders. The cleavage between high-level military leaders and the most militant Maoist leaders of the Central Cultural Revolution Small Group in Peking sharpened. Some military leaders were criticized and even removed from office. Many local military leaders with long and close ties with Party bureaucrats were particularly resistant to domination by revolutionaries outside the army. As attacks were expanded, more people felt threatened, and there was a danger that some cadres might combine with local military groups to resist the Cultural Revolution. This seemed to be true in such areas as Szechwan, Yunnan, and Kwangtung. The July 20th incident in Wuhan was the most striking instance, as leaders from the Central Cultural Revolution Small Group were actually held by local military leaders. This incident and its aftermath marked a turning point. Afterwards the Maoists were forced to make concessions to military leaders in order to prevent even more chaotic conditions and more open rebellion.

In the early weeks following the Wuhan Incident, the militant Maoists did try to tighten their control over rebellious military leaders.
When the two leaders who had been held in Wuhan were released and
returned to Peking, they were celebrated as heroes. Chiang Ch'ing
violently attacked some army leaders and encouraged Red Guards to
take up arms. Lin Piao attempted to clamp down on regional military
commanders, and outside troops were sent into Kwangtung to quiet the
disorder. Nevertheless the disorder reached such a peak that, by the
end of August, the militant Maoists had to back down. On September 5,
the authorities in Peking issued an order that no outsiders were to occupy
military installations and that no mass organizations could confiscate
army weapons. Chiang Ch'ing directed the revolutionaries to curb their
excessive revolutionary zeal, and Chairman Mao made a tour of troubled
provinces to encourage the revolutionaries to accept restraints. The
army was given explicit authority to keep peace and curb the revolutionaries when necessary, an authority that was far more explicit and detailed than anything since April. Since September the army leadership
has held the most important power positions, both at the central and
local levels. Government bureaucrats like Chou En-lai and Ch'en Yi,
who had been on the defensive since April, were cleared and returned to
prominence. Chiang Ch'ing's power was reduced, and leading militant
propagandists like Wang Li and Kuan Feng who had been attacking the
army and government bureaucrats, were purged. From April until August, these propagandists on the Central Cultural Revolution Small Group
had been riding high, but after September they lost out. Compromises
had to be made in order to get the army to move in to keep order, and
the army leaders were able to reduce the power of those who had been
attacking them since April.

Beginning in September the effort to form more stable ruling
organs, abandoned in February when the revolutionaries appeared too
weak, was revived. The basic principle to be followed in the leading
organs at each level was again the "Three Way Alliances," the combination of army leaders, former cadres, and revolutionaries. At each level
of administration new leadership groups were formed combining these
three groups but with the army clearly at the top.

In the spring, revolutionary committees had been formed in several places, but after their formation changes of personnel were required.
In the fall, because it was clear that conditions remained very unstable,
the new leadership groups at each level were not designated as "Revolutionary Committees" but only as "Provisional Revolutionary Committees."
As battles over composition quieted and membership was stabilized, pro-

visional committees gradually achieved permanent status.

New groups were formed when a small leadership group was selected by the leaders in Peking for each province and this group woula in turn select other members. Similarly, leadership groups constituting "Provincial Revolutionary Committees" were formed in the municipalities and counties within the province. These committees would in turn select members of the full "Provisional Revolutionary Committee" and the leaders for "Provisional Revolutionary Committees" for all the major political, economic, educational, cultural and social organizations within the locality.

The basic problem confronting these new revolutionary committees was to reunite in their organization enemies who had fought against each other during the Cultural Revolution. Red Guard students who had attacked bourgeois teachers now had serve with them. Party members had to work alongside the revolutionary rebels who had stormed their headquarters only a few months earlier. Cadres felt reluctant to return to work for fear that attacks might be resumed. However, the main burden of adjustment fell on the former revolutionaries who were the most undisciplined, few of whom were qualified to assume important positions. Just as the Communist guerrillas after Liberation had complained about serving under former Kuomintang bureaucrats, so many Red Guards and revolutionary rebels felt betrayed when they had to serve under cadres they had been called upon to attack only a few months earlier.

There was no easy solution for revolutionary committees trying to overcome the sharp cleavages between factions. Immediately after Liberation when guerrilla units were returned from the mountains and were united into a large uniform organization, they were accused of "mountain-topism." In the fall of 1967, this charge was heard again as leaders of various factions were accused of "mountain-topism." The immediate task confronting army leaders of revolutionary committees everywhere was personnel selection, determining who could be given positions of responsibility. The selection process inevitably involved negotiating with the various factions because large factions poorly represented in the new committees might continue the open feuding. Some army leaders found it simpler to work only with certain factions, avoiding the tedious problems of coalition government, but orders from higher levels clearly specified that they should not side with one faction but form an alliance. As in any campaign, all sides were bombarded with slogans. During this period the essence of the slogans was that everyone was to struggle against self-interest, criticize bourgeois revisionism, and accept the leadership of the military. Although the Thought of Mao Tse-tung became a cult from the beginning of the Cultural Revolution, in this new period the study of Mao took a new form and emphasized a new content. At each work unit, army representatives brought together members of different factions to study Mao's works with emphasis on public service and overcoming selfishness. In the context of praising the devotion of Chairman Mao and revolutionary martyrs to the national cause, members of all factions were called upon to pledge their willingness to forget their personal and factional interests, i.e., to accept the new organizations. Various sanctions, not always specified, awaited those who were slow to renounce self-interest.

The new alliances centered around the place of work. In the period of great liaison in late 1966 and early 1967, alliances were still being formed among various groups from many different cities and work units, but in the fall of 1967, alliances were ordinarily restricted to the people within a given work unit.

Once the provisional revolutionary committees were established, they were essentially grafted on to the top of the existing organization whether political, economic, educational, cultural, or social. The old leadership was replaced but at the lower levels cadres and administrators were for the most part retained, with a few revolutionaries added. Once the new committee had been formed, all the old personnel entered into group discussions where they had to demonstrate their willingness to repudiate revisionism and the leading Party figures accused of revisionism. Those who passed the test were allowed to remain on in the new organization along with the new input of military men and young revolutionaries.

Shake-ups were generally greater among the higher level organizations, especially at the large regional and provincial levels. They were greatest in the Party organization, but they were also frequent in government and educational organs. They were least severe in economic units and in rural areas. Aside from a few top Party leaders at every level who were subject to unremitting criticism, an attempt was made to persuade most cadres to confess. If they would not do so they were dismissed. The effect was to create a new leadership group and a slightly readjusted membership in most organizations throughout the society.

The Party was the most powerful political structure before the Cultural Revolution but the decimation of the Party organization was enormously disruptive. Most of the top Party leaders at all the levels from Party committees on up were severely criticized. Many lost their jobs, and a few were killed or committed suicide. Many Party committees had not functioned since mid-1966. Some Party members undoubtedly maintained contact with each other even in the midst of the worst attacks, but the key authority at all levels since mid-1966 was the military or the ad hoc Cultural Revolution groups. Once the new revolutionary committees began forming in the fall of 1967, an attempt was made to begin rebuilding the Party. It was announced that Party branches everywhere would resume their regular organizational meeting and that one of their first tasks was to assist in the rectification of the thoughts of the members in line with the repudiations of revisionism. By late October it was already announced that the 9th Party Congress, the first since 1956, was to be planned for late 1968. It is intended that some young revolutionaries would be selected to become probationary members of the Party, but this work of rebuilding has not yet begun on any sizeable scale. Although Party organs within the army have been given the responsibility for reviving regular Party meetings, there is no evidence that meetings have been resumed to any substantial degree.

To summarize, beginning in September 1967, there was a serious attempt to rebuild local political structures. By the end of 1967, the work of forming revolutionary committees was only partially completed and it was clear that even the task of selecting members for these committees would continue well into 1968. In the meantime, the possibility of factional in-fighting remains. There is great competition between factions over representation in the new alliance and over the severity of criticism and punishment their members are to receive. It is clear that the factions best represented in the leadership of the new committees will be able to maintain their influence and to criticize more of the opposition. Thus from late 1967 to the present (mid-1968) there have been frequent struggles everywhere, verbal and physical, and in some cases chaos. Serious struggles are still taking place but, compared to the events of the summer of 1967, they should be viewed in the context of rebuilding the organizations.

To date, all major rectification campaigns have begun with attacks on prominent figures and in the end tapered off to include a low-keyed rectification of ordinary workers and peasants. It is low-keyed in that the emphasis is on verbal criticism and persuasion rather than purging and physical punishment. The anti-rightist campaign of 1957 in Party and intellectual circles ended with a rural socialist campaign for consolidating the rural economy. Beginning in late 1967, as personnel adjustments were taking place in the lower levels of society, there was, in effect, a socialist education campaign which accompanied this readjustment. Making use of prominent campaign themes, rural propagandists are linking repudiation of Liu Shao-ch'i with repudiation of the bourgeois path. Thus the attack on Liu in the countryside is a vehicle for strengthening loyalty to the collective.

The Impact. The disruptions caused by the Cultural Revolution extended to virtually every phase of life in China and every major urban area. Our limited information prevents generalizations about the nature of disruptions, but a few preliminary interpretations do seem, on the basis of partial evidence, to be warranted.

During the Cultural Revolution, the severe attacks on the leadership made any kind of planning and decision-making difficult at best. Many organizations had to muddle through on the basis of old plans. Because of vulnerability to sabotage, the part of the economy most severely damaged was transportation and communication. Mining facilities were also in some places seriously damaged, which in turn affected other sectors of the economy. It is not possible to estimate the extent of damage, but it is known that exports declined at least several percentage points between 1966 and 1967, which suggests that output declined and/or the distribution of goods was disrupted, although not so badly as in the Great Leap Forward. Special care was taken to avoid disruption in areas vital to national defense. It appears that nuclear weapons work and defense industries were not seriously disturbed even in the summer of 1967. Agriculture, being less vulnerable to sabotage, suffered less damage and the excellent weather conditions may have boosted agricultural production during 1967 to an all-time peak. Agricultural collections were undoubtedly interfered with, and the Red Guards did disrupt rural work and appropriate grain from the farms on the outskirts of the major cities and along highways they traveled. The disorders seem to have had least impact in the relatively isolated and mountainous areas.

Although the economic damage has had a more direct and immediate impact, the greatest real damage was to education. As Mao put it, the economic transformation of organizations was essentially completed several years ago, and it only remains to change the superstructure. Hence, far more intensive reforms have been attempted or planned in the sphere of education than in economics. Schools were closed in the early summer of 1966, and it was not until February 1967, that primary schools began reopening. Middle schools began reopening in March but it was not until the fall of 1967, that middle school and college students began returning on a sizeable scale, and as of now (mid-1968) not only are few institutions of higher learning in operation, but many have not even made basic decisions about new curriculum. It is impossible to estimate how many students continued to study on their own or in informal schools, in schools operated by factories, business establishments or scientific academies during the Cultural Revolution, but it is clear that formal education beyond the primary stage was at a virtual standstill for well over a year, and had not yet resumed normal activity by the end of the year. Despite threats, many teachers were reluctant to return in the fall of 1967, to face their former critics. Many Red Guard groups which had taken over the schools in late 1966, were reluctant to give up their new-found power and in some cases their headquarters which were often located in schools.

The heightening of tensions, resulting disorders, and a weakened system of control provided more opportunity for petty criminals to take advantage of the lax situation for more market violations, looting, and illegal travel. The violent atmosphere prevailing during the height of the Cultural Revolution led to increased criminal violence. Red Guards ordered to return home could take advantage of their armbands to live off the local population. The Red Guard movements throughout the country combined with general disorder made it difficult to control population movements. One of the most serious problems was the difficulty of keeping young people in the rural areas when they would much prefer to migrate to the cities. Social control has been particularly difficult not only in border areas such as Sinkiang, Mongolia, and Yunnan, but also in areas such as Fukien, Shantung, and Kwangtung, where opposition was especially strong.

Aside from the immediate disorder, one effect of the heightened cleavages has been to create a greater sensitivity to political pressures. As the political struggle polarized and increased in severity, both the Maoists and the Party bureaucrats have tried to broaden their base of support. During the earlier period of outward unanimity the Party was under little pressure to compromise with local demands, but when Party bureaucrats and Maoists or various revolutionary factions are competing for support they can improve their position by making concessions to various groups of the population. For example, the Party bureaucrats appealed to workers by offering higher wages and pensions, while the Maoists countered by labeling the appeal "bourgeois economism." In turn, the Maoists criticized the bourgeois approach of opponents who hired contract labor but refused to offer a continuing salary when contracts were not available. The Maoists further appealed to peasants by blaming Party bureaucrats for the large gap in living standards between

rural and urban areas. The Maoists also appealed to the students from
poor backgrounds who resented the successes of the bourgeois children
moving on to higher and better schools. Both sides made concessions
to localists against outsiders, and, in the best Chinese political tradition,
both sides tried to use cleavages in the enemy ranks to recruit support
to their own side. With various factions competing for popular support,
there are more opportunities for representing special interests vis-à-vis
officials. In short, political cleavages have helped to broaden the base
of political power beyond the official hierarchy and to create more effective pressure groups.

Another side effect of the Cultural Revolution has been the open
airing of problems never previously acknowledged. Naturally as problems were exposed they were blamed on the other side, but their mere
admission of difficulties was nonetheless new. There was, for example,
complete repudiation of the excessively optimistic statistics used during
the Great Leap Forward. There was more frank recognition of the seriousness of the urban-rural gap. The waste and extravagence of elite
cadres and the special education facilities for their children were frankly
discussed. The existence of cliques and clique organization of leaders
was revealed. In South China, the Canton Railway Station incident of
June 1, 1962, and the escape of many refugees to Hong Kong in early
1962, was mentioned in the press for the first time. Before the Cultural
Revolution, difficulties were not mentioned, or, at best, discussed elip-
tically. During the Cultural Revolution, however, as cleavages sharpened,
the issues and problems which had separated opposing factions also came
out into the open.

Prospects

As local organizations are rebuilt over the next months and possibly years, one can expect continuing low-grade conflict and in some
cases more severe conflict. Most of the personnel for the provisional
revolutionary committees at the provincial, municipal, and in many
cases the county level have been selected, and by early 1968 some of
the provisional committees were becoming permanent. However, lower
level revolutionary committees in the factories, commercial establishments, educational institutions, mass organizations, and communes had
not been completely selected. Cadres who were not selected for membership or who were purged have not yet been entirely neutralized and
some still may be able to stir up resistance among their friends and
followers. The level of sabotage and physical conflicts at the end of the
year was not as high as in the summer of 1967, but the possibility of

passive resistance through absenteeism or slowdowns remains a serious problem.

Only a small portion of the Red Guards and revolutionary rebels can be selected for membership in new revolutionary committees or for youth league or Party membership. In the new alliances it is natural that the old cadres, because of their superior knowledge and experience, are often in stronger positions and reassert their old authority. For this reason many of the revolutionaries still feel betrayed by the reorganization and are afraid that they may suffer eventually at the hands of the cadres they formerly attacked. Many of them, therefore, have continued their attacks to the bitter end in hopes of forcing a more favorable compromise and because they see only a very grim future if they submit to the new leadership.

As a result, many ex-revolutionaries are not willing to give up the revolution, and this is true at higher as well as lower levels. Many Maoists fear that the revolution is being diluted by the old cadres staffing the revolutionary committees. There is little likelihood that the most prominent Party leaders criticized so thoroughly during the Cultural Revolution will return to positions of great power, but there is a danger that their successors will not differ greatly from them. The strategy of the Maoist leaders is to permit the new committees to form, but to nudge them occasionally by criticizing from above or by encouraging revolutionaries to attack from below. This strategy, of forming new committees while attempting to push them to the left, perpetuates tension with occasional outbreaks of violence, even after the organizations have achieved permanent status.

Reorganization at the lower levels of the countryside is not being pushed as hard as at higher levels. The leadership turnover in the countryside is minor compared to the heavy turnover in the winter of 1960. The association of poor and lower-middle peasants under the leadership of the militia, is able to stir up considerable criticism of cadres and wealthier peasants, but thus far there is no evidence that such criticisms of the bourgeois will assume the proportions it did during the "four cleanups" campaign in 1965.

One cannot rule out the possibility that the Maoists will again mount a major attack on newly emerging cadres and revolutionary committees for being too revisionist, but current problems are so great that it seems unlikely they will risk plunging the country into open conflict so soon again. The basic conflicts remain, though temporarily submerged.

Organizational rebuilding is likely to be slow at best. In view of the difficulties of planning the Party congress originally scheduled for 1963, one
would expect that it will be postponed again beyond the announced date of
late 1968.

In the short run the army is the only institution with the power
and authority to keep order and a balance between various factions. As
in the early period after takeover, the governing structure is essentially
a military occupation. In the early 1950's the military gradually retired
from the local political scene as peace was restored. Some soldiers
were discharged in order to retain their important positions as civilians,
while others left political positions to return to exclusively military tasks.
It is likely that this same process will be repeated now.

Once reorganization has been completed, the Maoists will probably urge some policy changes, especially in education. Mao has already announced his intention of writing new textbooks, abolishing examinations, shortening the number of years required for graduation, and
giving greater consideration to poor children even if they are not prop-
erly qualified. Many teachers are reluctant to return to school not only
because of the presence of students who formerly attacked them, but
because of the danger of being criticized for errors they might again un-
knowingly commit. In many schools the regime is confronted with a
painful dilemma. It would like schools to reopen, but it will take some
time to complete the reform of textbooks and materials. In the meantime teachers are reluctant to teach with the available teaching materials
since this might open them to criticism after new materials become
available. However, these new educational materials will have to be
written by new alliances, and clearly the process will not be an easy one.

Although the Maoists have been highly critical of the excessive
privatism in the countryside, during the Cultural Revolution the official
press said that Mao was himself responsible for the "Sixty Articles on
Agriculture." Since these "Sixty Articles" permitted private plots, private rural handicrafts, and private markets, fundamental structural
change in rural organization seems unlikely. No doubt in view of the
criticism of excessive capitalism in rural areas, there will probably be
greater supervision of private activities to assure that they do not interfere with the peasants' obligation to the collective.

In the economic sphere, aside from the announced intentions of
reducing the importance of "bourgeois incentives" and of simplifying the
administration by getting rid of excess personnel, it is unlikely that

there will be major new directions even after the consolidation of the new revolutionary committees. One cannot, however, expect rapid economic progress because of the disruptions of the last few years.

The wounds opened in the course of the Cultural Revolution will not heal easily, and in line with long-standing Chinese practices, many cadres will quietly submit while waiting for opportunities to "settle accounts." Disruption of the almost sacred Party authority will make it impossible for any succeeding political structure to command the unquestioned obedience it once had. The citizenry will be much more cautious in following the directives of constituted authority.

It is difficult for outside observers to get a precise sense of the seriousness of the current disorders. China has not by any means reverted to warlordism, but on the other hand the turmoil is obviously more serious than the current urban violence in the United States. On the one hand, Mao is sufficiently in control that no newspaper or radio ever directly and openly opposed Mao. It would seem that even Chiang Kai-shek is aware that he would not have enough local support to undertake serious penetration into the mainland. The regime has sufficient control that it is able to patrol its borders and prevent the escape of refugees. It has sufficient control to hold a trade fair attended by several thousand foreigners, in one of the more troubled cities, without a serious incident. On the other hand, there have been sizeable armed clashes involving large numbers of people, and the situation has not by any means stabilized. Millions of students, called upon to submit to authorities they rebelled against only a year before, constitute a source of dissatisfaction not easily brought under control. If there is a lesson of the Cultural Revolution, it is the potential disruption that can be caused as a result of high-level Party disagreements in which one leader takes his case to the masses. Such disagreements have not disappeared, and no outsider can predict the course they might take in the future.

The Cultural Revolution as originally conceived has not accomplished its major objectives. Bureaucratism, elitism, and selfishness have not disappeared. In the Great Leap Forward the utopian Maoists pushed their vision to the point of destroying the economy before turning back. In the great Cultural Revolution they have pursued revolution to the point of destroying the political fabric, and have consequently had to revert to many pre-Cultural Revolution political structures. The organizations temporarily used to purge the old Party officials, the Red Guards and the revolutionary rebels, have given way to more permanent political structures not unlike those of earlier years. The leaders of the Cultural Revolution were acutely critical of how Chinese society had failed to live up to the original revolutionary goals, but in the end they too had to compromise with their original goals. In the long run it may be possible to rebuild a Party not too different in structure from the early Party, but it is unlikely that it will again enjoy the unquestioned prestige and command the unquestioned obedience that it once did. In the mean- time, having damaged the moral basis of authority, the leaders in Peking have no choice but to rely on the army to maintain order by force.

Printed and bound by CPI Group (UK) Ltd, Croydon, CR0 4YY

13/04/2025

14656507-0004